FAITH, HUMOR, AND PARADOX

FAITH, HUMOR, AND PARADOX

Ignacio L. Götz

Westport, Connecticut
London

Library of Congress Cataloging-in-Publication Data

Götz, Ignacio L.
    Faith, humor, and paradox / Ignacio L. Götz.
        Includes bibliographical references and index.
        ISBN 0–275–97895–8 (alk. paper)
        1. Religion—Philosophy.   2. Religion—Humor.   3. Faith.   4. Paradox.   I. Title.
    BL51.G6854 2002
    210—dc21   2002029769

British Library Cataloguing in Publication Data is available.

Library of Congress Catalog Card Number: 2002029769
ISBN: 0–275–97895–8

First published in 2002

Praeger Publishers, 88 Post Road West, Westport, CT 06881
An imprint of Greenwood Publishing Group, Inc.
www.praeger.com

Printed in the United States of America

The paper used in this book complies with the
Permanent Paper Standard issued by the National
Information Standards Organization (Z39.48–1984).

10 9 8 7 6 5 4 3 2 1

As soon as Christ went down into
the water he came out laughing.
The Gospel of Philip

God deliver us from somber saints!
Saint Teresa of Ávila

Contents

Acknowledgments

Many sources have flowed together to give rise to this book, and their confluence spans many decades. With the passage of years it has become almost impossible for me to ascertain which idea came from which source. They have merged and mixed in my mind like the waters of many rivers flowing gently into the one sea. It is as if many voices had joined in chorus, and as happens when a choir sings, the individual voices are submerged in the joint sound of the whole. Still, I know the fountain springs. Like a conductor, I have before me the music score: I can identify the strains. I feel, therefore, that I should recognize with gratitude the source of ideas whose influence has been formative, and these are, mostly, my teachers, Peter De Letter, Jacques Dupuis, and Jules Volckaert. My colleague, Joanne P. Taylor, introduced me to the cultural dimensions of humor; Bill Orr made sure I did not misunderstand Gödel; and my wife, Katherine Götz, courageously ploughed through the manuscript and offered many suggestions.

I have been blessed with a dedicated and understanding editor in James T. Sabin, of Praeger Publishers, and my copy editor, Katie Chase, was ever vigilant and helpful.

Besides these, grateful acknowledgment is made to the following publisher for permission to reprint (upon payment of a fee) previously published material:

Paulist Press, for permission to quote from *Early Islamic Mysticism*, edited by Michael A. Sells. Copyright © 1996. Used with permission of Paulist Press.

Introduction

We live in a secular age, an age whose gods dwell in the marketplace, whose messengers are shining machines that sow destruction from the heights of the empyrean or from the depths lorded over by Leviathan. We live in an age that has enthroned the powers of reason in the shrines once reserved for the cult of numinous deities. We live in an age that worships numbers, that despises inexactitude — the age of precision watches, computers, and calculations correct to the last .02 percent of the binomial curve. This age has been a long time aborning. Henry Adams already envisioned it in the worshipful attitude he saw in the faces of visitors at the Great Exposition in 1900, enthralled by the awesome spectacle of the whirring dynamos in the Gallery of Machines.[1]

Ours is also an age that avoids risk and substitutes for it the appearance of daring. Kierkegaard already knew it.[2] We have no swimmers who simply and straightforwardly plumb the depths of uncharted waters. Instead we have divers who dazzle us with their complicated pirouettes before plunging into the certified safe waters below. Enterprise has given way to security, and hope to planning. It is too much to expect anyone to risk anything when mere appearance of danger can be just as exhilarating to the public.

In this context it is almost impossible to speak seriously of faith, for faith involves the taking of risks. We live in an age of reason, and reason guarantees security. In an address to the Philosophical Clubs of Yale and Brown Universities in 1896, William James felt he had to justify the human right to believe, that is, to assent beyond the boundaries of logic and empirical evidence — such was the temper of the times.[3] A few decades later Alfred Jules Ayer could state unequivocally that faith statements were nonsensical, since they did not pass muster under the principle of empirical verifiability.[4] If there is no God at the bottom of a test tube, there is no need of faith — strange reasoning, indeed. If science knows everything (or if everything is theoretically knowable), there is no room for mystery. If everything is planned there is no place for risk, and hope is elbowed out of the way. In Peter Berger's words, "we are, whether we like it or not, in a situation in which transcendence has been reduced to a rumor."[5] Faith, which is risk before the mystery, is a mere dreamer's dream. How, then, could the case be made for the religious significance of humor? How could humor be proved significant in relation to something as insignificant as faith? Writing on April 30, 1944, Dietrich Bonhoeffer asked, "How do we speak of God without religion, i.e., without the temporally-influenced presuppositions of metaphysics, inwardness, and so on? How do we speak . . . in a secular fashion of God?"[6] I should add that it is almost impossible today to speak of humor, for all we seem to know is entertainment and canned laughter.

Given this context, I have chosen to begin with a secular paradigm. Faith must don a disguise without ceasing to be faith. The paradigm, mathematical and linguistic, is one way of establishing the structure of belief in secular garb. It is a way of showing, where the secular mind least expects it, that however rational they be, logic and mathematics end up being paradoxical, and that this paradoxicality is the very basis for the growth of science — it provides the structure for all scientific revolutions. And, wonder of wonders, this same paradoxicality is at the root of religious faith and of humor.

PARADOX + SPIRIT = FAITH

In one of his books, *Spirit and Existence*, Michael Gelven writes that "to be spiritual means to think of oneself in terms of a reality which is beyond one's private limitations,"[7] and then he goes on to claim that to be spiritual is essentially paradoxical because "in order to understand the nature of spirit I must first recognize that I cannot understand. Spirit is that which is not understandable."[8]

Gelven defines paradox — and this definition will suffice for the moment — as a mode of thinking in which the truth we seek is possible only because of a conflict of some sort.[9] There are different kinds of conflicts, such as contradiction, counterintuition, falsehoods, but these generally destroy the truth. Paradoxes, on the other hand, preserve the truth because the truth is apprehended only while the paradox lasts; the truth exists precisely in the conflict that we call paradox. Paradoxes, Gelven says, "are not resolved or dismissed; they are absorbed or embraced, and only in so doing can the paradox become a source of illumination."[10] Now, if spirit is not understandable, it could be either nonsense or a mystery (as I shall explain in Chapter 1), but to claim it as mystery constitutes the paradox. Now, holding to the mystery even though it is paradoxical is what faith is, which is openness to the mystery. It can be seen, then, that of its very nature faith is connected with paradox.

However, one must guard against the desire to claim that everything that is inexplicable is automatically paradoxical and therefore must be believed. "There are . . . many falsehoods," says Gelven, "lying behind that mystical veil of ignorance which we . . . do not want to accept merely because they are mysterious,"[11] though I confess that I know many people who seem attracted by what they do not understand if it is said or written with sufficient authority or in obfuscating enough language as to appear to be truthful. A lot of esotericism commands a following merely because its members are unwilling to question or lack the knowledge required to raise issues of credibility. Thus, a lot of what passes for faith is just plain ignorance, though it may satisfy some basic need of the believer; but psychological need is no warrant for belief.

THE LAUGHTER OF JESUS

Secularists disdain talk about religious faith and the facile comedies of the day know nothing about gallows humor. A different kind of argument is usually raised by Christians who know little about the historical conditions in which the life of Jesus transpired and who take the Gospels — even the silences in it — literally. If Jesus did not laugh, they argue, why should they? Fundamentalism is ripe soil for this kind of obscurantism.

Not too long ago Umberto Eco wrote a mediaeval murder mystery in which the solution hinges on the alleged preservation of Aristotle's "lost" book on comedy, a copy of which is in the monastery library. An old librarian in the monastery, Brother Jorge, is bent on keeping the "lost" book lost because he fears that, if Aristotle's philosophical weight is brought to bear on the importance of humor, everything Christianity has fought for will be lost. Laughter, he argues, "is weakness, corruption, the foolishness of our flesh. It is the peasant's entertainment, the drunkard's license."[12] This is the point of view of those who argue that Jesus never laughed; on the contrary, he promised heaven to the sad, to those who mourn,[13] and actually lamented for those who laugh; for in the after-life, he is quoted as saying, those who laugh shall mourn and weep.[14]

Commenting on these passages, St. John Chrysostom insisted that Jesus, according to the Gospels, never laughed or smiled "even a little."[15] And he added:

> That is why Christ says so much to us about mourning, and blesses those who mourn, and calls those who laugh wretched. For this is not the theater of laughter, neither did we come together for this intent, that we may give way to immoderate mirth, but that we may groan, and by this groaning inherit a kingdom.[16]

St. Augustine said in a sermon, "People laugh and weep, and it is a matter for weeping that they laugh."[17]

We do not know, of course, whether or not Jesus laughed. The fact that the Gospels do not say he did means nothing, for they, in turn, do not say he did not. The notion of a mirthless Jesus is a construct developed by commentators based on the fact that the redactors of Jesus's sayings and deeds did not bother to depict a laughing Jesus, prompted, perhaps, by the memory of the crucifixion[18] and the Roman military occupation of Palestine. They had, in other words, their own agenda. On the other hand, Bruce Chilton has argued that, based on solid evidence from ancient times, it is legitimate to maintain that Jesus was a jovial man who substituted convivial feasting for the asceticism of the Baptist's immersion:

> He left that part of John's program behind in favor of his own practice of festive celebration. . . . The Galileans understood, both emotionally and intellectually, what these meals meant. Their land was clean and acceptable to God. They were pure and forgiven. Their bread was an emblem of God's kingdom.
>
> As their enthusiasm for Jesus' banquets increased, he worked less and less and feasted more. . . . His inner compulsion to celebrate the divine presence, to press all who would listen to enjoy God's power in the luscious fruit of Galilean soil, usurped his loyalty to family and convention.[19]

It is hardly believable that Jesus would have participated in such joyous feasts and never have laughed. In fact, the *Gospel of Philip* portrays Jesus as coming out of the baptismal water in which John had immersed him laughing at everything in the world, and promising that whoever laughs in the same way will be saved.[20] The Gnostics, interestingly, made a distinction between the Jesus who died on the cross (the *Jesus patibilis*) and the real, living Jesus, and they attributed laughter to this real Jesus, not to his fleshly likeness. They also argued that not everyone "saw" the difference,[21] a sobering thought for those who oppose laughter. Much later on, the monastic movement considered laughter undignified and offensive in the monks, for it disrupted the silence of the monastery. It was also seen as a sign of lack of self-control, and it was, therefore, deemed reprehensible.[22] But what is there to fear in holy laughter?

THE TEN OXHERDING PICTURES

The connection of spirit and humor is evident in other traditions. In all traditions recognizing the importance of enlightenment, self-analysis has led to the mapping of progress toward it. Not that the steps necessarily lead to the culmination of the search, but that when enlightenment occurs, it appears to have followed a recognizable sequence of steps or stages. Philosophical, artistic, and scientific literatures in the West speak of preparation, incubation, insight, and creation (or, in science, verification). Mystical traditions East and West have produced exhaustive analyses of four similar stages, generally termed purification (*via purgativa*), progressive illumination (with intervals of "darkness") (*via illuminativa*), ecstasy (*via unitiva*), and a return to action or praxis. In the twenty-five hundred years from Patanjali (reputed author of the *Yoga Sutra*) to psychologist Catherine Patrick, probably no other aspect of human experience has been studied as carefully and as extensively as this path to vision.

Zen is no exception. Kaku-an Shi-en (*ca.* 1100-1200), a Zen master of the Rinzai School, first described these stages in ten pictures, using an ox as the symbol for the eternal, primal nature of the self, our Buddha-mind.[23] Thus the "Ten Oxherding Pictures" came into being. Kaku-an, however, referred to another Zen master called Seikyo, probably a contemporary, who had used five pictures to describe the path to *satori*. According to Suzuki,[24] there is another set of six pictures by Zen master Jitoku Ki. The number of pictures grew until the current ten, and commentaries to accompany each picture have been written on the verse captions by Pu-ming.

In most of the sets, the tenth picture depicts an enlightened man, rotund and jolly, marching merrily to the marketplace. It is as if the masters wished to say that *satori* need not lead to the demise of laughter. In fact, to emphasize the point, some sets paint the master sitting on the ox backwards![25]

HUMOR AND FAITH

The intrusion of humor in religion has been chronicled even in secular settings. In his historical novel, *The Devils of Loudun*, Aldous Huxley comments how during the seventeenth century the efforts of the royals and the rich to cover themselves with grandeur and pomp, were almost always marred by grotesque occurrences and sloppy procedures. He cites the example of *La Grande Mademoiselle*, first cousin of Louis XIV, whose dead body was embalmed in pieces — "here the head and there a limb or two, here the heart and there the entrails."

> These last were so badly embalmed that, even after treatment, they went on fermenting. The gases of putrefaction accumulated and the porphyry urn containing the viscera became a kind of anatomic bomb, which suddenly exploded, in the middle of the funeral service, to the horror and dismay of all present.[26]

And, to be sure, to the laughter of all. For to be laughed at was the price to be paid by those whose self-inflation did not lift them above the heads of all the rest. Nothing new in this. We have always enjoyed accounts of the foibles of great people — "the bromidrosis of dukes and marshals," as Huxley puts it, the missteps and mishits of President Gerald Ford — and the extant instructions for courtiers, from ancient times to the present, bear witness to the fact that great efforts were spent trying to prevent such amusing catastrophes.

The comic cannot be denied. When God solemnly told Abraham that he would have a child in his old age, and that his wife Sarah would therefore become pregnant (even though she had entered menopause[27]), Sarah laughed despite the seriousness of the occasion; Moses had to be reminded to take his sandals off when he came before the Burning Bush;[28] and "Oi vey" was all Isaiah could say when he found himself in the Temple in the midst of a divine theophany.[29] Similarly, the gods laughed uproariously when Hephaistos caught his wife Aphrodite in bed with Ares;[30] and a maid from Thrace is said to have burst into laughter when she saw Thales fall in a hole because he was walking looking at the stars.[31] Dante titled his great poem *Commedia* because it began badly and ended well and because it was written in such plain language that even the scullery maids could understand;[32] and Erasmus wrote his *Praise of Folly* while he suffered the pains of gallstones on his way to visit Sir Thomas More.[33]

P. L. Travers has left us an unforgettable description of a visit to a waterfall near a Zen monastery in Japan. The night of the visit the waterfall was frozen like "a shawl of marble, silent, not a stir," while the moon's light shone brightly in the dark night. Moved by the sight, the reverent tourists murmured, "Wonderful! Wonderful!" Right at that moment a prancing monk stood by them, clasping his hands and "gazing with unction at the waterfall, caricaturing their rapture," exclaiming, "Two-derful! Three-derful! Four-derful! Five-derful! Six!" while he hurried away.[34] Nothing wrong in this, though we often have difficulty with laughter in holy places. No wonder the powers that be have systematically suppressed carnivals and similar festivities all over the world, for they dislike the exaggerations of celebrations and the unbearable lightness of being to be found in humor. Hence the question, again, how to talk about humor and faith in such a way as to command a hearing.

THE COURT JESTER

In *King Lear*, Act I, Scene 4, Shakespeare has the Fool define himself as one who takes "one's part that's out of favour," as he criticizes Lear for the way he dealt with his daughters; and he plays this role of critic to the point that Lear warns him with a threat of whipping. The criticism is pointed, accurate, even though it is couched in obloquy and pronounced, after all, by a fool. The Fool, thus, is to be seen as an in-between figure, sitting by the side of the King, specifically labeled a fool, yet capable of speaking to the King and of stating what other courtiers often think but are unable to articulate under penalty of whipping, banishment, and death. The Fool, in other words, personifies the fanciful spirit that, according to Huizinga, plays "on the border-line between jest and earnest."[35]

Fools were different from buffoons, the comics who made a living entertaining the opulent, from ancient Greece to modern Europe and America. Nothing was at stake for them except the joke, and in households where life bordered on the boring, they gained ready entrance and a good meal. They still grace club dinners and college campuses as stand-up comics, and even though so few take to heart the role of the social and political critic, most are after the easy laugh that guarantees their paycheck.

Describing the citizens of Utopia, More said that "they set great store by fools" and forbade doing them any harm or not laughing at their jokes, for fear that they would stop being funny.[36] In the Baghdad of Hārūn al-Rashīd (ninth century), the comic Bahlul played this role to perfection. Many stories are told of him, of which I choose a short one:

> Once Bahlul was included among the guests at a sumptuous banquet in the house of a wealthy merchant. Among the delicacies that were offered was a dish of Damascene nougat. "What is this?" asked a fellow diner. "I don't know," said Bahlul, "but I have heard people say that the most exquisite thing on earth is a bath. This, I think, must be a bath."[37]

But the real Fool — the "professional" Fool, as one of Burns's Jolly Beggars calls himself [38] — the Jester, was much more than an entertainer. Mostly men (though records show the existence of women court jesters, such as Mathurine, in the French court), they used their wit not only for fun but as a counterfoil to the seriousness of the court. According to Hyers,

> It was one of the virtues of the Middle Ages to have recognized most clearly that every king needs a court jester, a part of whose function is not only to make the king laugh, but to make him laugh at himself. In the grotesque form of the jester, the king in all his pompous authority and power is revealed to his courtiers and to himself as also something of a clown. . . . The sacredness of the royal person and the sacrality of his rule (the "divine right") require the profane person and mock rule of the court fool in order to preserve that delicate dialectical balance between holiness and humor, on either side of which, in the socio-political realm, are the pitfalls of tyranny and anarchy.[39]

Hyers maintains that the court Fool is an example as well as a reminder of the relationship between the sacred and the comic, a relationship he terms dialectical; because, he says,

> contrary to common prejudice, the sacred object or act requires not only the responses customarily associated with holy matters — reverence, awe, solemnity, etc. — but the responses customarily looked upon as in some degree inappropriate to the sacrality of the sacred, the responses of comedy and laughter.[40]

Without this relationship, the sacred tends to become pompous and, eventually, despotic and fanatical; and the comic, similarly, tends to become frivolous and inconsequential.

THE TRICKSTER

The vision of the monk, a holy man, prancing about delighted with his joke, calls to mind the "trickster," the universal embodiment of the prankish spirit. These figures were mostly male, for we have lived in patriarchy for the past several thousand years, but some female tricksters exist, as I shall show below in the case of Baubo.[41] Generally, the trickster is a deceiver and a fool all in one. He is Loki of the Norse myths, Hermes the playful Messenger, Krishna the Butter Thief, Coyote, Baubo the obscene Crone, and Sheila-na-gig the Flasher.

The infant Krishna was constantly up to all kinds of tricks, as the villagers complained to Yaśodā, his mother. He would go to the houses of the people early in the morning before the milking of the cows and let loose the calves, who would then drink all the milk, so the people got nothing; he would steal the yogurt and butter wherever it was kept, and give it to the monkeys, and when these were satisfied and could eat no more, he would taunt the villagers saying, "Look, not even the monkeys like your butter and yogurt!"[42]

Coyote, too, was always up to all manner of tricks. Once he was challenged by a white man (*wasichu*) who thought nobody could get the better of him.

"Hey," he called out to Coyote, "let's see if you can outsmart me."

"I'm sorry," said Coyote, "but I can't do anything without my cheating medicine."

"Cheating medicine?" said the white man. "Well, go get it!"

"Oh, it's miles from here and I'm on foot; but if you lend me your fast horse I'll go get it."

"Ok, you can borrow the horse. Go home and get your cheating medicine."

"Well, it's more difficult than that. Your horse doesn't know me; but if you lend me your clothes, he'll let me ride him."

"Ok, here are my clothes. Get on the horse and go get your medicine."

So Coyote rode off with the white man's clothes and his horse.[43]

Finally, I shall mention the story of Baubo, of which we have different versions. It is connected with that variant of the myth of the abduction of Persephone which has Hades rape her and carry her down to the Underworld. In anger and grief, Demeter, her mother, withdrew from the world and refused to let any plant germinate in the ground. To make her laugh and thus restore some measure of fertility to the earth, old Baubo lifted up her skirts and exposed her pudenda![44]

Now, all these trickster figures are connected with the sacred in some way, perhaps indicating from time immemorial the necessity of conceiving humor at the heart of the holy.

WHERE TO BEGIN

Given the considerations briefly explained above, it should be clear why this book takes a circuitous route to its goal. This is the purpose of the excursion into the realms of logic and mathematics that will occupy Chapter 1 — to prepare the ground for an analysis of faith in Chapters 2, 3, 4, and 5. It is thus an effort to begin with the prejudice of the age and to show that it, too, like all idols, has feet of clay. Chapter 6 will discuss the character of humor, and Chapter 7 is a note on frivolity. Chapter 8 will finally put together humor and faith. A Conclusion will round up the argument.

Many topics of the utmost importance are touched on in this book — theological and philosophical ideas that have preoccupied great minds through the ages. Where outstanding and lengthy treatises have been written about them, I often deal with them in one or two short sections. I do not want to appear to belittle all those efforts, nor do I think that my brief comments are the ultimate word. In many cases they are not even a summary, but I believe I have said enough, in most cases, to give a sense of the importance of the issue and where my sympathies lie in the matter under discussion.

NOTES

1. Henry Adams, *The Education of Henry Adams* (New York: The Modern Library, 1931), p. 380.

2. Søren Kierkegaard, *The Present Age* (New York: Harper Torchbooks, 1962).

3. William James, "The Will to Believe," in *Essays in Pragmatism* (New York: Hafner Publishing Co., 1966).

4. Alfred J. Ayer, *Language, Truth and Logic* (New York: Dover Publications, n. d.).

5. Peter Berger, *A Rumor of Angels* (Garden City, NY: Doubleday, 1969), p. 120.

6. Dietrich Bonhoeffer, *Letters and Papers from Prison* (New York: Macmillan, 1962), p. 164.

7. Michael Gelven, *Spirit and Existence* (Notre Dame, IN: University of Notre Dame Press, 1990), p. 18.

8. Ibid., p. 24.

9. Ibid., p. 23.

10. Ibid., p. 23.

11. Ibid., p. 33.

12. Umberto Eco, *The Name of the Rose* (New York: Warner Books, 1984), p. 576.

13. *Matthew* 5:4 and *Luke* 6:21.

14. *Luke* 6:25.

15. St. John Chrysostome, *Homilies on the Gospel of Matthew* (New York: Catholic University of America Press, 1998; reprint of the Post-Nicene Christian Library edition of 1888), VI.6.

16. Ibid., VI.5.

17. St. Augustine, *Sermo 31*. *Opera Omnia*, in *Patrologiae cursus completus*, Series Latina, J. P. Migne, ed. (Paris: Garnier, 1844-1855), Vol. 38, col. 194.

18. Wayne A. Meeks, *The Origins of Christian Morality* (New Haven: CT: Yale University Press, 1993), pp. 61 *ff.* and 86 *ff.*

19. Bruce Chilton, *Rabbi Jesus. An Intimate Biography* (New York: Doubleday, 2000), pp. 75-76.

20. *Gospel of Philip* 74:29 and 35, in *The Nag Hammadi Library*, James M. Robinson, ed. (San Francisco: Harper & Row, 1981), p. 145. For other similar passages, see Ricky Alan Mayotte, *The Complete Jesus* (South Royalton, VT: Steerforth Press, 1997), pp. 149-150. Also John Dart, *The Jesus of Heresy and History: The Discovery and Significance of the Nag Hammadi Gnostic Library in English* (New York: Harper & Row, 1988).

21. *The Apocalypse of Peter* 82:27 to 83:3, in *The Nag Hammadi Library*, pp. 344-345.

22. See Karl-Josef Kuschel, *Laughter: A Theological Reflection* (New York: Continuuum, 1994), p. 44. Kuschel does a good job detailing the attitudes toward laughter in the Hebrew Bible as well as the Christian Scriptures.

23. Philip Kapleau, *The Three Pillars of Zen* (Boston: Beacon Press, 1965), p. 301.

24. Daisetz Teitaro Suzuki, *Manual of Zen Buddhism* (New York: Grove Press, Inc., 1960), p. 128.

25. For example, see the painting, "The Zen Master Seiogyu," by Kano Naizen (1517-1616).

26. Aldous Huxley, *The Devils of Loudun* (New York: Harper Colophon, 1965), p. 263.

27. *Genesis* 18:11. See Ted Cohen, *Jokes: Philosophical Thoughts on Joking Matters* (Chicago: The University of Chicago Press, 1999), p. 52.

28. *Exodus* 3:5.

29. *Isaiah* 6:5.

30. *The Odyssey* VIII. 326 *ff.*, in *Great Books of the Western World*, Robert M. Hutchins, ed. (Chicago: Encyclopaedia Britannica, 1952).

31. Plato, *Theaetetus* 174A, in *The Dialogues of Plato*, B. Jowett, trans. (Oxford: Oxford University Press, 1871).

32. Calling the *Comedy* "divine," as is common today, destroys the essence of the mediaeval notion of comedy, which is the contrast between hell and heaven.

33. In Latin, the title *Moriae Encomium* is a pun on More's name. *The Praise of Folly* is equally *The Praise of More*.

34. P. L. Travers, "Zen Moments," *Parabola* 12:4 (November, 1987), p. 18.

35. Johan Huizinga, *Homo Ludens: A Study of the Play-Element in Culture* (Boston: Beacon Press, 1966), p. 5.

36. Sir Thomas More, *Utopia*, Book II, in *The Harvard Classics*, Charles W. Eliot, ed. (New York: P. F. Collier & Son, Co., 1965), p. 211.

37. Inea Bushnaq, transl. & ed., *Arab Folktales* (New York: Pantheon Books, 1986), p. 276.

38. Robert Burns, *The Jolly Beggars*, in *The Harvard Classics*, p. 125.

39. M. Conrad Hyers, "The Dialectic of the Sacred and the Comic," *Cross Currents* 19 (Winter 1969), p. 72.

40. Ibid.

41. Lewis Hyde, *Trickster Makes This World* (New York: Farrar, Straus & Giroux, 1998), p. 8 and Appendix 2.

42. A. C. Bhaktivedanta Swami Prabhupāda, *Krishna, the Supreme Personality of Godhead* (London: Bhaktivedanta Book Trust, 1986), pp. 81-82.

43. Richard Erdoes and Alfonso Ortiz, eds., *American Indian Myths and Legends* (New York: Pantheon Books, 1984), p. 342.

44. Hyde, *Trickster*, pp. 336-337.

1

The Nature of Paradox

We shall begin with a look at a class of statements whose structure is peculiar in that they seem to defy full comprehension. We call them paradoxes; that is, statements that move along the borders of logic, neither within it nor against it, but just on the periphery, as it were. The first thing to do is to inquire into the nature of these statements, for they will lead us eventually to the very nature of the act of faith.

THE NATURE OF PARADOX

There are statements which, according to Hofstadter, rudely violate "the usually assumed dichotomy of statements into true and false" because if you tentatively think one of them is true, then "it immediately backfires on you and makes you think it is false. But once you have decided it is false, a similar backfiring returns you to the idea that it must be true."[1] As long as one remains locked within this system of mutually exclusive truths and falsehoods, one is caught in a kind of maze. This maze is what is called paradox: within its system, there is no "solution" possible.

Paradoxes must meet three conditions. As statements they must be (1) self-evidently self-referential, (2) self-contradictory, and (3) infinitely circular.[2] This means there may be paradox-like statements that satisfy one or two of the criteria but not a third, or that fulfill the three but in a weak form. These may be complex or ambiguous pronouncements, not paradoxes.[3] Statements such as "This sentence has five words" are clearly self-referential but not paradoxical, for they are not self-contradictory or infinitely circular. On the other hand, the following sign

DON'T READ
THIS SIGN

is self-referential, self-contradictory, and even circular, but not infinitely so. It is therefore a weaker kind of paradox. The same may be said of the so-called Derrida's Paradox: "There is nothing outside the text."

Let us dwell for a moment on this third requirement. Circularity involves the proving of a statement by reference to another statement that itself requires proof by the first or previous statement, and so on *ad infinitum*. Infinite circularity had been invoked in Aristotle's "third man argument" as a way to close off debate. In fact, says Aristotle, "it is lack of education not to know that it is necessary to seek demonstration of some propositions and not of others. For there cannot be a demonstration of everything altogether; there would then be an infinite regress, and hence there would still be no final demonstration."[4] The appeal here is to common sense. Any attempt to prove everything would result in infinite regress trying to prove the basis of the proof itself — and therefore no proof would be forthcoming. But there is an implication in Aristotle's statement that is worth considering, namely, that some propositions may be unprovable though true. For obviously, the fact of infinite circularity merely entails unprovability, not falsehood. Self-reference means that the proof of a proposition involves reference to the proposition itself that one wants to prove — the so-called vicious circle. Self-contradiction, on the other hand, refers to the requirement that a system, in order to be complete, must include both positive propositions and their opposites, thus violating the principle of consistency.

Self-reference and contradiction can be easily captured in the following example adapted from Tarski. Take the sentence, "This statement is not true." This statement shall be represented by the letter "s." Therefore we have the following:

(1) "s" is true if, and only if "This statement is not true."

But since empirically we can observe an identity between "s" and the statement it represents, we have:

(2) "s" is identical with the sentence it represents.

Given (2), then, and given the principle of identity (A = A), it follows that we can replace in (1) the expression "This statement" by the symbol "s." As a result we have the following:

(3) "s" is true if, and only if, "s" is not true.[5]

This is, of course, self-contradictory, though paradoxically so.

Kurt Gödel's undecidability theorem starts from a similar paradox. Gödel constructed a formula that proved that no system (including explanatory systems) can be both comprehensive and consistent, for in striving to be comprehensive it would have to account for itself, and it cannot do that and be consistent. Wittgenstein had already come to a similar conclusion in 1921. He had argued in *Tractatus* 3.332, that "no proposition can make a statement about itself, because a propositional sign cannot be contained in itself."[6] And he added:

The reason why a function cannot be its own argument is that the sign for a function already contains the prototype of its argument, and it cannot contain itself.

For let us suppose that the function $F(fx)$ could be its own argument: in that case there would be a proposition '$F(F(fx))$', in which the outer function F and the inner function F must have different meanings, since the inner one has the form $ø(fx)$ and the outer has the form $\psi(ø(fx))$. Only the letter 'F' is common to the two functions, but the letter by itself signifies nothing.[7]

Gödel's proof, which appeared a few years later, can be stated as follows. Take a formula A, so that

(1) A means A is unprovable; (A, that is, is what it is if, and only if, it is not provable).

Further assume that

(2) False formulas are not provable.

Then A cannot be false because if it were it would have to be not-notprovable (i.e., provable). It would then be false but provable, which would contradict (2). However, A could be true and unprovable. For even though it may be granted that all provable formulas are true, the reverse is not necessarily correct: not all true formulas are provable. If this were so, then all unprovable formulas would be false. But this is clearly not so because of (1). A then is true but unprovable.

What is demonstrated thus is that no system can be both consistent and complete. To be complete within the bounds set for itself, it would have to prove itself (that is, be self-referential). It cannot do that, and therefore it is incomplete: "the system is incomplete in the sense that it fails to afford proof of every formula which is true."[8] Gödel's second theorem applied this incompleteness characteristic to all complex systems. This is also the conclusion arrived at by Tarski.[9] In consequence, no formal, systemic description of nature can be complete, since at some point in its search for completeness it must seek to account for itself — it must involve self-reference — at which point it becomes self-contradictory. Now, since such statements, undecidable within the system, may still be true (though unprovable), the possibility exists that they are provable within a larger, richer system. In other words, undecidability within a system opens the door to a new dimension.

Two conclusions follow from the above exposition. First, thinking is essentially a search for the open-ended because in fact thinking strives to find statements that are not provable within the system. Second, the passage to an ulterior dimension takes place as the logical possibilities of the system are explored in detail and exhausted.

That thinking is essentially looking for open-endedness is an inescapable conclusion. Given the fundamental incompleteness of systems, thinking must be seen as a search for the openness to whatever beckons beyond the limits of systems with their proofs and demonstrations.[10] "There is often an alternative way of arranging available information," writes de Bono.

> This means that there can be a switch over to another arrangement. Usually this switch over is sudden. If the switch over is temporary it gives rise to humor [as we shall explain below]. If the switch over is permanent it gives rise to insight. It is interesting that the reaction to an insight solution is often laughter even when there is nothing funny about the solution itself.[11]

We shall return to this connection with humor later.

Before the switch-over, however, thinking is concerned with the systematic examination and classification of the data until all the instances are elucidated and all the possibilities explored. This thinking often goes by the name of research. It is, indeed, research: the searching again and again for a comprehensive explanation, which in turn will point to a passage out; it is the repeated exploration of the known terrain in expectation of a new discovery.

Research is often painstaking, slow, boring. Ortega calls it "inertial thinking," for in it the mind, under the impulse of a notion or idea evident in itself, continues indefinitely, almost mechanically, to think in the same direction. Ortega gives this as the reason why Hegel calls ordinary mathematical thinking *entäussertes Denken*, alienated or externalized thinking, for in it one need not attend to the operations one is performing. Inertia does not mean lack of movement but perseverance in one state, be it of rest or of motion.[12]

When this inertial thinking gives way to "wakeful thinking" (*el pensar alerta*), discovery occurs. Writes Bassui to the Abbess of Shinryu-ji: "When you persistently try to understand [with the intellect] what is beyond the domain of intellect, you are bound to reach a dead end, completely baffled. But push on!"[13] According to Kuhn, this is what must take place if a change in scientific paradigm is to happen. One elaborates the data according to one set of rules until anomalies occur that require the elaboration of another set.[14] The process repeats itself indefinitely, for reality remains forever refractory to absolute, final, and comprehensive systematization. Yet it is only through systematic efforts at comprehensibility that new and unexplored panoramas are discovered. The object of research, therefore, is not the total systematization of reality — this can never be accomplished — but the building of ever better standpoints from which to catch a glimpse of truth deprived of the protection of proof, of reality naked and unadorned; or, as Adorno puts it, of reality "suspended and frail."[15]

The passage from one system to another as elucidated above can be viewed from two different perspectives, namely from below (as it were) and from above. Generally, the scientific model is an "ascending" one. Exhausting a system entails rising to a higher one. Thus Teilhard de Chardin envisages evolution of the "psychic" as a growth, both in intensity and geography, that leads eventually to a critical point — at the apex of a pyramid, as it were. Here the entire balance of the stage is upset, and although only an infinitesimal change may have occurred, a new level has been reached. An example is given:

> When water is heated to boiling point under normal pressure, and one goes on heating it, the first thing that follows — without change in temperature — is a

tumultuous expansion of freed and vaporised molecules. . . . By the end of the Tertiary era, the Psychical temperature in the cellular world had been rising for more than 500 million years. . . . When the anthropoid, so to speak, had been brought "mentally" to boiling point, some further calories were added. . . . No more was needed for the whole inner equilibrium to be upset. . . . Outwardly, almost nothing in the organs had changed. But in depth, a great revolution had taken place: consciousness was now leaping and boiling . . . and was capable of perceiving itself in the concentrated simplicity of its faculties.[16]

Human consciousness is depicted here as the "flecting" or turning over upon itself of anthropoid psychism at a level higher than that achieved by the earlier anthropoids.

On the other hand, the "descending" mode functions differently. In the *Republic*, Book VI, Plato argues similarly from the realm of mathematics to that of the Forms. Mathematics, we say, *rests on* assumptions, postulates, hypotheses. But Plato saw mathematics, rather, as *hanging from* the theses; that is, the Forms. A hypothesis, literally, is "below-the-thesis" — it does not uphold itself but is upheld by something higher, more perfect and permanent, certain, and eminently intelligible: the Forms. And while the movement is here from inferior to superior, the Forms clearly can be seen also as the ultimate condition of intelligibility. From their exalted perspective one looks down, as it were. Contemplating them one contemplates the entire world — and therefore contemplating them, in a certain sense, suffices. Christianity places the Forms in God's essence; hence God is said to know everything in and through his own essence, the ultimate exemplar of everything created. Even the Faustian Mothers, according to Goethe, see nothing but the eternal Forms.[17] Thus every newly discovered realm may be seen also, as it were, from above, as the condition of everything that has led up to it and is now dependent on it for its own intelligibility. Jaspers writes that "we always have something which the understanding cannot grasp but which is decisive for our certainty of being."[18]

There is in Scholasticism a notion that is relevant here. This is the notion of *potentia oboedientialis*, obediencial potency. It involves the concept of a being that possesses a potential that cannot be actualized by the being itself in question. The potential can be actualized only from the outside, as it were. This potential is like the water of a well which cannot of itself pour out of the well but can be brought out (that is, has the potential to be brought out) by an outside agent with a bucket.

This notion was developed to explain the phenomenon of grace. To maintain that human beings can become united to God is to maintain that they are *capaces infiniti*. But to maintain that this potential can be actualized by human beings themselves would entail the notion that salvation is totally self-administered. It is also to maintain that the creature is of itself capable of attaining the uncreated and that finitude can comprehend infinitude through its own unaided powers. Such self-actualization would render the creature supreme and would at the same time destroy the hegemony of the divine. Hence the notion of *grace*; that is, gift: salvation is *given*, granted. Grace, thus, is vouchsafed, but it encounters a ready recipient — or at least a recipient that may be rendered ready by the very grace it is to receive. Grace is a call the creature is capable of answering (that is, has the potential of answering), but only when the call is uttered. This potential, therefore, is not actualized until the call has been issued and accepted.

This notion today seems alien to many due to the prevailing emphasis on *self-actualization*. For Marxists and Existentialists alike, humans are their own makers, the architects of their own destinies. To think otherwise is to surrender the essential autonomy of the person. But clearly there is a sense in which human life is an answer to some beyond, whether this beyond be that of another Person, of love, of life, or of fate. It may also be an answer to the call of Being. At any rate, such a concept involves an openness to a beyond that issues a call. The call does not come except to a hearing that is constituted as hearing in the very happening of the answering; it comes as a filling of an openness that is constituted as opening in the very act of its fulfillment. The transcending of a system, therefore, may be seen as a bursting forth of concealed energies within — very much as a seed bursts forth or germinates at warm touch of the sun — or as an emanation drawn out by a powerful outside force — very much as a magnet draws to itself all the pins from a pin cushion.

When the beyond opened up by paradox is seen in this double light, it is easy to understand why contradictions and antinomies cannot be considered mere frivolities and pastimes of the mind. They are the threshold of discovery, or the prelude to being addressed. Tarski states unequivocally that "it would be quite wrong and dangerous from the standpoint of scientific progress to depreciate the importance" of these antinomies "and to treat them as jokes and sophistries,"[19] and Jaspers considers the task of philosophy "not the removal of its circles and contradictions, but rather the bringing of them to light in order to see whether they are significant or merely empty circles."[20]

One must therefore emphasize the importance of the paradox and the need to maintain its openness. Some thinkers have sought to do away with paradoxes, to dissolve them by a careful analysis of the use of language. For them paradoxes are meaningless propositions, and their lack of meaning arises from a careless use of language. Thus the task of the logician, says Waismann, "does not consist in giving an answer to them, but in not letting them arise."[21] Waismann, interestingly, bases his work on Lord Russell's *Principia Mathematica* and opts for the dissolution of the paradox. This was the general position of the logical positivists. Russell himself felt uncomfortable around paradoxes. On the other hand, Gödel, whose original work was drawn from the same source, came to different conclusions, as is well known.

UNAMUNO AND PARADOX

In his comments on Hegel's *Wissenschaft der Logik*, Unamuno wrote that "the opposites of dialectic exist together and their only possible union is the process of existence itself."[22] That is, polar notions are not true at the expense of each other; rather, they are true only when they are present together, and any effort to prefer one over the other is a betrayal of the very reality of existing.

Claims such as this are paradoxical, though perhaps in a weaker sense of this term (as explained above). Unamuno saw paradox essentially as a revolt against the logicians, as a way to escape the tyranny of logic. He relished paradox. "Since people have said that I delight in paradox," he wrote, "I am not going to let them down."[23]   In *Niebla* he wrote: "I need discussion; without discussion and contradiction I am not alive."[24] Again: "If you want, reader X, to read something coherent, transparent and clear; tied logically; having a beginning, a middle, and an end; and that aims at teaching you something, look for it elsewhere, not here."[25] No wonder many critics have found him "too fond of paradox, too critical of logic."[26]

By paradox Unamuno clearly excluded utterances which are merely irrational or nonsensical. He expressed this forcefully shortly before his death in his confrontation with General Millán Astray. He disdained any servile acceptance or blind assent to absurd propositions simply because they sounded good.

In defining paradox he followed etymology. "Paradox," he wrote,

> is every idea, or better, every expression of ideas that departs from common sense. "Para–" means deviation, what lies outside; "–doxa" means opinion.
>
> All right, so it is what goes against common sense . . . .
>
> Not against, for then it would be *antidoxa* and not *paradoxa*; it is not what goes against the strong mainstream [of common opinion] but what diverges from it.[27]

For Unamuno, therefore, paradox "is the most energetic means of presenting a truth. A nail must be driven on its point, not on its head; a truth is like a nail, a wedge in the fabric of your ideas."[28] Again: "Paradox is the most efficacious means of progress. . . . The history of human thought could be reduced to the conflict and mutual interplay between common sense and proper sense, between platitude and paradox."[29] For Unamuno, paradox is a way to avoid the constricting strictures of logic. To have analyzed paradox more systematically would have been to succumb to the control of logic from which he was trying to escape.

At the same time, paradox is worlds removed from the "flexidoxy" of contemporary relativists who, in a desperate attempt to escape the Enlightenment search for metanarratives, have given up the quest for truth at all.

EPIMENIDES THE CRETAN

Perhaps the most famous of all true paradoxes is that attributed to Epimenides. Epimenides (*ca.* 600 B.C.E.) seems to have been a Cretan from Knossos. Legends about him abound and the few extant fragments attributed to him are of dubious genuineness. In fact some scholars maintain he did not exist, but that his "paradox" was invented by a certain Eubulides of Megara, the successor of Euclid. At any rate, the statement is quoted by St. Paul in his letter to Titus (1:12). It states that Epimenides maintained, "All Cretans are liars." This statement would not be particularly noteworthy were it not for the fact that Epimenides himself was a Cretan. Hence the statement has become famous. It is known as "The Liar's Paradox" — if the statement is true, then it must be false. We sense this intuitively: it does not seem possible that all Cretans should be liars. But how could this be known? "The falsity of the statement," argues Kleene, "requires that there has been, or will eventually be, a Cretan who at some time tells the truth."[30] Yet this solution seems inadequate since it is not verifiable in fact.

PARMENIDES AND ZEN

Other examples of ancient paradoxes can be stated briefly. Nagarjuna (*ca.* 200 C.E.) was one of the main intellectual exponent of Mahāyāna Buddhism. He literally created a system in order to get rid of a system. Every system, he maintained, terminates in inconsistencies. It is therefore nullified. But it cannot be totally negated since its negation would entail an act of another system, and wisdom recoils from endless affirmation and negation (the "infinite regress" of Aristotle) — it recoils from infinite circularity. The mind is thus pushed beyond systems to the things themselves in their essential reality. This is what Nagarjuna called "the Void," though he was quick to add, "it cannot be called void or not void, or both or neither, but in order to indicate it, it is called the Void."[31]

In other words, reality is what it is — to call it anything is to fit it into a system. But systems have been shown to be self-contradictory when it comes to naming reality. Therefore the system must open up to what is beyond it, reality itself. This is the basic insight, the "transcendental wisdom." Hence the paradoxical nature of statements common in the Mahāyāna tradition (and in Zen, its intellectual and religious successor):

> The disciple Subhūti said: "Profound, O Venerable One, is the perfect Transcendental Wisdom."
> Quoth the Venerable One: "Abysmally profound, like the space of the universe, O, Subhūti, is the perfect Transcendental Wisdom."
> The disciple Subhūti said again: "Difficult to be attained through Awakening, is the perfect Transcendental Wisdom, O Venerable One."
> Quoth the Venerable One: "That is the reason, O Subhūti, why no one ever attains it through Awakening."[32]

And at this point both of them must have burst laughing.

The enlightenment that is called *satori* in Zen is prepared, but not guaranteed, by different techniques. The techniques vary from counting breaths to *shikan-taza* (literally, "just sitting"). A notorious technique is that of the *kōan*, "that great baffler of [logical] reasoning," as Suzuki calls it.[33] The *kōan* (Chinese *kung-an*) was first developed in China by Huang-lung (1002-1069). It was later introduced to Japan and became firmly established there through the work of Hakuin (1686-1769), a master of the Rinzai school.

One of the fundamental purposes of the *kōan* is the breaking down of the barriers erected by our analytical reason so that reality may be apprehended. The mind that looks for reasons, for logical solutions, is an obstacle to enlightenment, since it operates within the confines of a partial logical system. Therefore the hold of logic must be broken, and the *kōan* is a good method for achieving this result. A similar function is served by the fantastic formulas at the beginning of some folk tales: "Once there was and once there wasn't, in the old days, when the sieve was in the straw, when camels were barbers and the cock was a town crier. . . ." Nan

Runde comments: "the nonsense rhyme throws the logical mind off balance, taking us into a realm accessible only to the imaginal, intuitive mind, the mind of the poet and the child."[34]

The kōans used by the masters have arisen out of their own experiences; hence they can be solved only experientially, as it were: *solvuntur ambulando*! But perhaps the real point is that they cannot be really solved, because they are true paradoxes. They are logically intractable and incomprehensible. The only way to "solve" them is to step beyond them. One of the most famous ones is the kōan known as Jōshu's "Mu": A monk asked Master Jōshu, "Does a dog have Buddha nature?" Jōshu answered, "Mu!"

"Mu" can be translated as "No," or "Nothing." But the meaning is irrelevant. Any effort to find meaning through discursive reasoning is bound to end nowhere, because the question is paradoxical in nature. If the answer were "Yes," it would be false (contradictory) because it would demean the nature of enlightenment (Buddha nature); if the answer were "No," then Buddha nature would not be universally present. We have here once more Gödel's theorem: if the statement is comprehensive it cannot be consistent. The logic breaks down. A serious, prolonged, unremitting, and effortful consideration of this paradox will hopefully lead the seeker to the realization that the question is answerable only in "another dimension" — that is, that it is not answerable at all. Such a realization is termed *satori*, enlightenment, and is the goal of Zen practice. Tai-in, a Korean Zen Master (*fl.* sixteenth century), gives the following recommendation:

> Keep the kōan always before your mind and never release the spirit of inquiry. As the inquiry goes on steadily and uninterruptedly you will come to see that there is no intellectual clue to the kōan, that it is altogether devoid of sense as you ordinarily understand that word, that it is entirely flat, devoid of taste, has nothing appetizing about it, and that you are beginning to have a certain feeling of uneasiness and impatience. When you come to this state it is the moment for you to cast aside the scabbard, throw yourself down into the abyss, and by so doing lay the foundation for Buddhahood [enlightenment] . . . . You will finally find yourself like an old rat [trying to escape] getting into the farthest corner of the barn where it suddenly perceives by veering clear round the way of escape.[35]

The paradox of the kōan on "Mu" is similar to the one old Parmenides pressed on the young Socrates in Plato's *Parmenides*. The young Socrates had expounded to the old master his hypothesis about "participation." The Forms are real archetypes of lower reality, says Socrates, an idea Parmenides finds interesting. "Did you think this out by yourself?" he asks Socrates. And when the young man acknowledges authorship, Parmenides proceeds to question him, pushing his arguments to paradoxical conclusions in an effort to disprove them through *reductio ad absurdum*.[36] The argument is direct. It is relatively easy to accept the existence of Forms of goodness and justice and beauty, says Parmenides. But are there Forms of man, of fire, of water? he asks. Socrates is less certain of that but concedes the point. However, when Parmenides presses him to assert that there are Forms of mud, hair, and dirt, Socrates cannot bring himself to assent. The dilemma is clear. If the Forms are to serve as universal archetypes of reality, there must be Forms of everything; but if there are forms of mud, this seems to demean their exalted status. Therefore, if the theory is comprehensive and universal, it is contradictory, Q.E.D.[37]

The purpose of the *Parmenides* does not seem to be to disprove Socrates's theory of participation (or for that matter Parmenides's monism). It is rather to show how any system, however profound and comprehensive — in fact, precisely because it seeks to be comprehensive — ends up in self-contradiction. Socrates acknowledges the paradox and his inability to dissolve it. Parmenides suggests that profounder insights will come with age, that wisdom will allow paradoxes to appear in a different light. And an aging Plato (who is really the thinker behind Socrates's words) admits that logical solution of the paradox is not the crucial point, for logic is too weak an instrument for the apprehension of reality,[38] a conclusion not unlike Gödel's second theorem even though formulated in a different manner.

CONCLUSION

The open-endedness of logical and mathematical systems is but one example of the openness of thinking. Science is full of specific instances. From the twelfth century on, for example, there were efforts to push beyond Eucledian geometry, culminating in the breakthroughs of the eighteenth and nineteenth centuries. "Through a point P outside a line, L, there can be drawn one, and only one, line parallel to L," said the Eucledian Fifth Postulate. "No," counter non-Eucledian geometricists, "through a point P outside a line, L, there can be drawn several lines parallel to L, at least two of which intersect L at infinity." And architects still build structures based on the former while engineers send astronauts to the moon based on the latter. Neither system alone encompasses or explains the totality of reality.

The same thing has happened with the mechanistic view of the Newtonian universe. For a century after its proposal it held undisputed sway, until Faraday and Maxwell began to push beyond the confines of its structure. Today the clockwork regularity and symmetry of Newtonian physics have been relativized. "If I live twenty years on earth while my identical twin brother travels through space at near the speed of light, we will both be the same age when he returns to earth," says common sense. "No," counters Einstein, "he will be younger, for time passes at different rates relative to the mass of the solids which attract it." Time, like space, has no absolute determination. Everything is relative to the distribution and configuration of matter in the universe.

A pattern becomes clear. A system — whether of logic, mathematics, or physics — emerges. Investigation and experimentation seek to bring all of reality under its purview: the mind yearns to make the system as comprehensive as possible. Exceptions arise and are quickly integrated into the system through modifications in it. But a point eventually comes when new data prove refractory, stubborn, indigestible, incapable of being assimilated within the system. At that point the possibility arises of explaining the data already accumulated within the system as well as the new material by means of another, higher, more comprehensive system. A leap takes place from one system to another, from one dimension to another, from one mode of reasoning to another. "Enlightenment always comes," says Mu-mon, "after the road of thinking is blocked."[39] Similarly, new systems arise after the explanatory capabilities of the old ones have been exhausted.

This is the secular paradigm I have been trying to elucidate. I must now proceed to show that the same mechanism is at work in the act of faith. The movements are the same whether we pass from one earthly system to another or from a human to a divine understanding of reality; or simply to an indefinite openness. The systems we pass on to may be different — in fact, they will be different. But the structure of the passing will be the same.

NOTES

1. Douglas R. Hofstadter, *Gödel, Escher, Bach* (New York: Basic Books, 1979), p. 17.

2. Patrick Hughes and George Brecht, *Vicious Circles and Infinity* (New York: Penguin Books, 1979), p. 1; Ignacio L. Götz, "Unamuno: Paradox and Humor," in *Selected Proceedings of the* Singularidad y Trascendencia *Conference*, Nora de Marval-McNair, ed. (Boulder: University of Colorado, 1990), p. 73.

3. Philip Wheelwright, *Heraclitus* (Princeton, NJ: Princeton University Press, 1959), p. 98.

4. Aristotle, *Metaphysics* IV. 4 [1006^a 5-8].

5. Alfred Tarski, "The Semantic Conception of Truth," in *Problems in the Philosophy of Language*, Thomas M. Olshewsky, ed. (New York: Holt, Rinehart & Winston, Inc., 1969), p. 585. Also Alfred Tarski, Andrzej Mostowski, and Raphael M. Robinson, *Undecidable Theories* (Amsterdam: North-Holland Publishing Co., 1968).

6. Ludwig Wittgenstein, *Tractatus Logico-Philosophicus* (London: Routledge & Kegan Paul, 1961), p. 31.

7. *Tractatus* 3.333, p. 31.

8. Stephen C. Kleene, *Introduction to Mathematics* (New York: D. Van Nostrand Co., Inc., 1952), p. 205. Also Raymond M. Smullyan, *What is the Name of This Book?* (Englewood Cliffs, NJ: Prentice-Hall, Inc., 1978), pp. 234-241. Gödel's argument is to be found in "Über formal unentscheidbare Sätze der *Principia Mathematica* und verwandter Systeme, I," *Monatshefte für Mathematik und Physik* 38 (1931): 173-198. See also Barkley Rosser, "An Informal Exposition of Proofs of Gödel's Theorems and Church's Theorem," *The Journal of Symbolic Logic* 4:2 (June, 1939): 53-60. See also Harry Gensler, *Gödel's Theorem Simplified* (Lanham, MD: University Press of America, 1984), and George Boolos, "Gödel's Second Incompleteness Theorem Explained in Words of One Syllable," *Mind* 103:409 (January, 1994): 1-3.

9. Jacob Bronowski, "The Logic of the Mind," *American Scientist* 54: 1 (March, 1966): 4-5.

10. Cf. Theodor Adorno, *Negative Dialectics* (New York: Seabury Press, 1973), p. 20 *ff.*

11. Edward de Bono, *Lateral Thinking: Creativity Step by Step* (New York: Harper Colophon, 1970), pp. 35-36.

12. José Ortega y Gasset, "A 'Veinte años de caza mayor' del Conde de Yebes," in *Obras Completas* (Madrid: Revista de Occidente, 1966), Vol. VI, p. 442.

13. Cited in Philip Kapleau, *The Three Pillars of Zen* (Boston: Beacon Press, 1966), p. 169.

14. Thomas S. Kuhn, *The Structure of Scientific Revolutions* (Chicago: The University of Chicago Press, 1970), pp. 52-53.

15. Adorno, *Negative Dialectics*, p. 34.

16. Pierre Teilhard de Chardin, *The Phenomenon of Man* (New York: Harper & Row, 1961), pp. 168-169.

17. Goethe, *Faust*, Part II, line 6290, in *Goethes Werke* (14 vols. Hamburg: Christian Wegner Verlag, 1948).

18. Karl Jaspers, *Reason and Existenz* (New York: The Noonday Press, 1957), p. 115.

19. Tarski, "The Semantic Conception of Truth," p. 586.

20. Jaspers, *Reason and Existenz*, p. 116.

21. Friedrich Waismann, *The Principles of Linguistic Philosophy* (New York: St. Martin's Press, 1965), p. 90.

22. U-1260, in Mario Valdés and María Elena de Valdés, *An Unamuno Source Book* (Toronto: University of Toronto Press, 1973), p. xxxiv.

23. "El resorte moral," in *Obras Completas*, Manuel García Blanco, ed. (Madrid: Herederos de Miguel de Unamuno, 1965), III, p. 278.

24. *Niebla*, en *Obras Completas*, II, p. 977.

25. "Ramplonería," *Obras Completas*, I, p. 1245.

26. Philip Phenix, "Unamuno on Love and Pedagogy," in *Existentialism and Phenomenology in Education*, David E. Denton, ed. (New York: Teachers College Press, 1974), p. 98.

27. *Monodiálogos*, "La paradoja," in *Obras Completas*, V, p. 973.

28. Ibid., p. 972.

29. *Contra esto y aquello*, "Un filósofo del sentido común," in *Obras Completas*, III, p. 551.

30. Kleene, *Introduction to Mathematics*, p. 39. See also Smullyan, *What is the Name of This Book?* p. 214 *ff.*; Jaspers, *Reason and Existenz*, p. 114.

31. *Madhyamika Shāstra* 15, 3, in *Āryanāgārjunīyam Madhyamika shāstram* (Vāranāsī: Bauddhabhāratī, 1983).

32. *Ashtasāhasrikā Prajñāpāramitā* 8, Edward Conze, transl. (Calcutta: Asiatic Society, 1970).

33. Daisetz T. Suzuki, *The Essentials of Zen Buddhism* (London: Rider & Co., 1963), p. 307.

34. Nan Runde, "At Home in the Land of the Little Green Waiting-Maid," *Parabola* 26:3 (August, 2001), p. 22.

35. *The Mirror for Zen Students* [1579], quoted by Suzuki, *Essentials*, pp. 302-303.

36. Plato, *Parmenides* 130, in *Great Books of the Western World*, Robert M. Hutchins, ed. (Chicago: Encyclopaedia Britannica, 1952).

37. Ibid.

38. Plato, *Letter VII* 343A.

39. *Mumonkan* 1, in Paul Reps, *Zen Flesh, Zen Bones* (New York: Doubleday Anchor, n. d.), p. 89.

2

Faith and Paradox

Like many people, I grew up thinking that belief and faith are one and the same thing; after all, I affirmed my belief "in God, the Father Almighty and in his only son, Jesus Christ"; I confessed also that I believed "in the resurrection of the dead and life everlasting," and I readily acknowledged that this was my faith. I knew that there were people of other faiths and I understood this to mean that they had other beliefs different from mine in which they believed with the same or even greater conviction, and that this was as it should be.

Later on I came to learn that the word "belief" was used in broader contexts, and that it designated states of mind characterizing knowledge of which the speakers weren't quite sure, but to which they gave allegiance.[1] Belief fell somewhere between opinion and knowledge. If you said you had an opinion, this meant you had considered the matter seriously and had formed a set of statements that summarized it and for which you had good reasons, but which were not strong enough to give you certainty, and certainty was the characteristic of states of mind in which you were positively sure. When you said, "I *know*," with an emphasis on the *know*, it meant you were sure of the matter, you knew with certainty. Belief, however, expressed some sense of comfort mixed with uncertainty but leaning toward certainty. "I believe that such-and-such is the case," was not just a matter of opinion; it expressed a nearness to certainty not present in opinion and a readiness to act on account of it,[2] and a certain commitment.

Furthermore, I also learned that belief and faith were terms quite reasonable in a secular context. You could believe in the future, in the honesty of another person, in the legitimacy of the democratic process; you could even believe that God believed in you, as Claude sang in *Hair*. All these seemed to be legitimate ways of speaking, and people understood each other when such expressions were used. If there was any problem it was with the content of religious faith, the things we said we believed, with which others disagreed, sometimes vehemently.

I also came to understand that there is a distinction between "belief *in*" (*credo in*) and "belief *that*" (*credo*), the former a matter of moral will, the latter a matter of intellect.[3] It also became apparent to me that over the centuries, in the West at least, "belief *in*" had slowly given in to "belief *that*" as the most important kind of faith. This may have been due to the growing interaction between Jews, Christians, and Muslims in the Middle Ages, a commerce that called for definition of differences rather than similarity of belief, a point that was more easily made by reference to dogmas and clearly delineated matters. This kind of emphasis has persisted into modern times, and it accounts, at least in part, for the rampant fanaticism we encounter today among adherents of all major religions.

TRADITIONAL DEFINITIONS

Religious faith can be defined as an assent because of the authority of a revealing God. This definition turns faith into an intellectual act and it places the emphasis, at least implicitly, on *what* is believed, though, again implicitly, what is believed is considered to be not evident or immediately present — that is, to be beyond reasonable evidence. Hence the introduction of a motive for believing, God's authority, who would not deceive us in presenting something for our belief which was not true. Obviously, God's authority is preferred to reason's because we are dealing with religious faith, not scientific belief. Faith, thus, is faith in God and in whatever God says must be believed. The ultimate reason for believing religiously is not evidence, but God.

Proponents of this view of faith acknowledge that this assent of faith takes place in a certain penumbra because the content is not sufficiently supported by reason or other evidence worthy of trust. By definition, *what* is believed is beyond reason; hence the need to introduce the authority of God as the motive for belief; that is, as the only force capable of bending the will to believe. At all events, if things are evident, it is not faith.

It is also argued that the assent of faith is given with certainty, not as opinion, but with the surety of true knowledge; and this even though rationally the evidence may not be there. Nevertheless, such an assent is considered to be free because there is no obligation (beyond a general moral one) to accept God's authority. There is need, therefore, of a specific act of the will to command the assent, since it is not necessitated by the reasonableness of the evidence. Still, as should be apparent, this understanding of faith emphasizes "belief *that*" over "belief *in*", and it is here, I think, that conflicts tend to arise.

An example, for me, was St. Paul's comments in *1 Corinthians* 1:18-31, where he maintained passionately a belief that Jews and Greeks considered foolish — namely, that God became human in Jesus. For a Jew, any divinization of humanity was anathema, and for the Greeks, the notion of an absolute, infinite being *becoming* and, moreover, becoming *finite*, was self-contradictory. Yet St. Paul insisted that if one had faith, if one had heard God's call, this belief, "a stumbling-block to Jews and folly to Greeks," possessed a saving power. In short, St. Paul presented the view that faith required confrontation with a paradox, the paradox of the God-man. The statement, "This man [Jesus] is God" is paradoxical because it is self-evidently self-referential: it refers to Jesus in applying to him two characteristics which, in the Jewish religion and in Greek philosophy, are mutually exclusive or self-contradictory, since in the Jewish religion God is the creator and we are his creatures and a creature cannot be both creature and creator of itself, and in Greek philosophy God, as absolute and infinite, cannot be non-absolute (i.e., relative) and finite, nor can he both *be* and *become* at the same time. This paradox became famous in Tertullian's formulation.

TERTULLIAN'S PARADOX

For centuries Tertullian's *Credo quia absurdum* has been taken as an illustration of the irrationality of the Christian faith — indeed, of *all* faith. Few commentators have paused to ask what Tertullian might have meant by the phrase, especially since he *never* actually wrote those exact words.

That Tertullian was *not* an irrationalist is easily proved by the powerful rationality of his entire output. Moreover, some scholars have maintained that Tertullian's argument about belief in the incarnation and crucifixion is not centered on the paradox *Credo quia absurdum*, but concerns, really, the claim that Jesus's crucifixion and death were not shameful just because Marcion had claimed they were; on the contrary: since Marcion was wrong anyway, what he affirmed as wrong must of necessity be right. Thus Barnes,[4] who claims that Tertullian's argument is purely rhetorical, and that the paradox is only apparent and of secondary or subsidiary importance.[5] On the other hand, B.A.O. Williams uses the paradox as an example of the pitfalls of religious language.[6]

Here I wish to argue, first, that, as explained above, paradox is not anti-reason, much less, irrational, but only a legitimate way of expressing certain unprovable truths (though the expressions may appear nonsensical); second, that there is not one paradox but two, though the first is subsumed under the second; finally, that Tertullian's statements *are* paradoxical because that is the only way faith statements can be expressed.

The Polemical Context

Marcion maintained that God had not been *born* as Jesus because, to begin with, Jesus did not have a true human body, since, according to Gnostic teaching, any union with matter would have been repugnant to the spirit. Jesus did "die" on the cross, but what perished there was a phantom body (*umbra, phantasma*). For orthodox Christianity, this was the heresy of Docetism. Against Marcion, Tertullian argued that, by showing himself as a human being in Jesus, God implicitly accepted birth, which is the common entrance into the world for all human beings.[7] Further, Tertullian argued that being born and dying on the cross, which the Docetists rejected as unbecoming to God, were *possible if willed by God*, and therefore were legitimate items of faith for the Christian.

Moreover, Tertullian's attack on Marcion's views took place in the context of Paul's statements in *1 Corinthians* 1:18-31 cited above, that "the doctrine of the cross is sheer folly," and that "God has made the wisdom of this world look foolish." For "as God in his wisdom willed it, the world failed to find him by its wisdom, and he chose to save those who have faith by the folly of the Gospel . . .

Christ nailed to the cross . . . a stumbling-block to Jews and folly to Greeks," but "wiser than human wisdom."[8]

Tertullian's text

A preliminary premise of Tertullian's argument is the assertion that "Nothing is impossible for God but what He does not will."[9] Tertullian maintains that, if God willed to be seen as human, he implicitly willed to be born, because all humans are born, and because, *if he willed it, it happened*, since he had the power to make it happen. While in this passage Tertullian is arguing primarily against the Docetism of Marcion, the premise has important implications for the argument that concerns us here. For, in placing will and not reason as the primary premiss, Tertullian undermined the argument that belief in the birth and death of God was irrational, since the point, clearly, is not rationality or making sense, but rather, whether or not God wills it. Given this premise, God's birth and death, however foolish according to the standard of reason, must be deemed possible according to the standards of an absolutely powerful will such as God's. The famous statements, then, follow:

> I am saved if I be not shamed of my Lord. . . . The Son of God was crucified: I am not ashamed because people must needs be ashamed of it [*Non pudet quia pudendum est*]. And the Son of God died: it must be believed because it is absurd [*Credendum est quia absurdum*]. And he was buried and rose again: the fact is certain because it is impossible [*Certum est quia impossibile est*].[10]

The key word in these statements is *quia*, "because." In both Latin and English the use of this conjunction is often ambiguous, especially following a negative clause (as it does in some of Tertullian's statements). Here, at least two meanings of the statements are discernible. Thus, "I am not shamed because people must needs be ashamed of it" can mean that people's being ashamed of this is no reason *for me* to be ashamed; or it can mean that since people are usually ashamed of such beliefs I will exult in them. Similarly, "it must be believed because it is absurd" can mean that since the belief is absurd, the only way for me to deal with it is through belief; or it can mean that I relish irrational belief. Finally, "the fact is certain because it is impossible" can mean that faith is the only way to achieve certainty vis-à-vis a seeming impossibility, or that one should enjoy belief in the impossible.

The statements have generally been interpreted in the latter sense in all three cases. Moreover, belief in the shameful, the absurd, and the impossible has been construed as paradoxical. Hence comes the use of the statements as proof of the irrationality of faith, it being assumed that paradox is to be eschewed. But such a reading is not altogether warranted, since everything Tertullian wrote seems to favor a different interpretation. Moreover, concentrating on the paradox of belief in the absurd and impossible obscures the real paradox to be found in the absurd and impossible statements *themselves* (namely, that God has become a man, has been born, and has died). Thus, belief in the absurd (the first paradox) dissolves into the God-Man paradox (the second one), which can only be dealt with by belief.

Perhaps the difference presented above between the two readings can be clarified by making a distinction between the *how* of belief and the *what* of belief.

Those who interpret the paradox as a statement of the irrationality of faith place the emphasis on the *what* of belief. Thus, they see Tertullian as claiming that faith is belief in what is shameful, absurd, and impossible regardless of the irrationality of such a belief, for faith relishes the irrational.[11] On the other hand, those who interpret the paradox as emphasizing the *how* of belief claim that Tertullian presents faith as the only way of assenting to paradoxical religious statements, thus going beyond the accepted, ordinary rational system in order to deal with data incapable of being brought within the system.

I think that this latter interpretation of the paradox is the only sensible one. I see Tertullian as the first theologian in Western Christianity to understand faith as a mode of assent beyond the reasonableness of proof and the feasibility of fact. In this he follows the suggestion of Paul, but as a theologian, he is the first one to confront squarely the groundlessness of faith. For him, faith lacks ultimate justification in reason. He is the first one to propose, albeit paradoxically, the existence of a realm of affirmation beyond the boundaries of logic and ordinary facticity. He is the first one to contend that faith is one of the possible answers to the absurd.[12] In a profound sense, he is the first one to understand the truly paradoxical nature of faith.

WILLIAM JAMES AND KIERKEGAARD

More recently, William James has claimed that faith is assent "in spite of the fact that our merely logical intellect may not have been coerced" by evidence.[13] In such instances, *"our passional nature not only lawfully may, but must, decide an option between propositions, whenever it is a genuine option that cannot by its nature be decided on intellectual grounds."*[14] Again, this is the case with paradox.

James emphasizes the role of the will in the case of faith, everything else being equal; but rather than ground this act of the will on the authority of God and the impossibility of his deceiving us, he has recourse to "our passional nature," the fact that we have a dimension of will that has force in certain well defined instances. Put differently, according to James, "our non-intellectual nature does influence our convictions,"[15] very much what Pascal meant when he proclaimed, "We know truth, not only by the reason, but also by the heart,"[16] a view Pascal derived from St. Augustine's "No one ever believes anything unless first he think it must be believed."[17] For James, then, "belief consists in an emotional reaction of the entire man on an object."[18] The conditions for the influx of "our passional nature" are those of paradox.

Such an understanding of faith is pushed almost to an extreme by Kierkegaard. In faith, he says, alongside the paradoxical nature of the object of belief itself, there is a dialectical opposition between subject and object, since the object does not necessitate assent. This opposition is overcome by the will to believe. The experience of this willful rush Kierkegaard called "the pathological proof."[19] Faith, then, is "an objective uncertainty, due to the repulsion of the absurd, held fast by the passion of inwardness."[20] The objective uncertainty, however, or paradox, is of a special kind, since it pertains to the divine mystery, of which the believer becomes aware beyond the paradox; for "nonsense . . . he [the believer] cannot believe against the understanding . . . but he makes so much use of the understanding that he becomes aware of the incomprehensible, and then holds to this, believing against the understanding."[21] The incomprehensible is, in fact, the *ultimate* or *absolute* paradox, but there must be a paradox or there is no faith: "If a believer answer the objection he is *eo ipso* not a believer."[22]

The paradoxical serves a double function, then, that of pointing to the limit of reason and that of arousing passion, the will to believe. Kierkegaard interprets reason's search for paradox as reason's search for its own limits — as reason's efforts to prove its own inadequacy vis-à-vis undecidability. "The supreme paradox of all thought," he wrote, "is the attempt to discover something that thought cannot think."[23] Faith arises in this context of paradox as the transcending of logic in a leap to believe.

WHAT FAITH *IS*

After all the preceding considerations and the passage of years, I have come to understand that faith, at least religious faith, is not so much concerned with the *whats* of dogmas and traditions as with the *Who* that is the ultimate object of faith, the One who grasps us as we take the "death-defying leap"[24] beyond reason. According to Augustine, "faith is the first thing that joins the soul to God."[25] Faith, as Tillich explained years ago, "is a total and centered act of the personal self, the act of unconditional, infinite and ultimate concern."[26] Faith is that act by which a person turns totally toward the infinite. It has little to do with dogmas, tenets, catechisms, doctrines, beliefs. It is essentially the person's openness to what ultimately matters.

The tenets of faith that we purport to believe are not the real thing, because, for the most part, we have striven to make them understandable to ourselves, thus depriving them of their paradoxical nature. In de Lubac's words, "the whole of dogma is . . . but a series of paradoxes, disconcerting to natural reason and requiring not an impossible proof but reflexive justification."[27] True faith, like true paradox, cannot be resolved or elucidated. In fact, this is why we believe, because we cannot understand yet yearn to love That which is beyond our understanding.

If anything, the paradoxical tenets of faith do for us what the *kōan* does for the Zen practitioner: they detach us from the rational[28] and propel us unto the mysterious that Otto called *mysterium tremendum* ("to be feared"), but which is, above all, *amandum* ("to be loved"). St. Augustine claimed that God created us to tend to Him, and that our hearts are restless until they rest in Him.[29] Faith opens up the gates to our restless hearts[30] that they may gallop swiftly to the grazing pastures of the great Horse Whisperer.

Following Kierkegaard, I have come to understand that faith unlocks the doors to an undiscovered country wherein dwells the Divine Incognito (as Barth named God),[31] the Beloved. Faith is the link to the Unknowable Presence about which we stammeringly affirm our articles of belief. In truth, dogma tells us little about the Divine, but whatever it tells links us to It beyond the very details of belief. These details, for whose truth we have killed millions of people, are truly secondary, for what is most important is the connection with the Divine opened to us in the act of faith. As a blind person comes to see by touching, we come to know by believing,[32] but what we know is not primarily the tenets of faith, but the Unfathomable beyond all utterances, the Indescribable behind all descriptions, toward Whom we speed ardently in love along the tracks laid down by faith. Faith, truly, is like a worm hole between our human/earthly dimension and that of the Divine. In faith, blind acrobats hurtling through circus heights, we somersault into the outstretched hands of the Beloved whose presence we sense and whose allure we feel, but Whom we cannot see. This was the fate of Psyche, the beautiful maiden whose lover, the divine Eros, came to her in the midst of blackest night, so that she heard his manly voice murmuring sweet nothings, felt his warm caresses, but was not permitted to gaze on his wondrous beauty — and therefore was ignorant of his true nature.[33]

"To have faith is to be in labor," wrote Abraham Heschel,[34] not the labor of understanding, nor the labor of discussion and encounter, but the labor of allowing oneself to be gripped by the widespread hands of God. In this process, to be concerned about the content of one's beliefs is a temptation, like being distracted by the flashes of photographers' cameras while performing a high-wire act. This is the theological danger, defining dogma at the expense of mystical union; for what does it profit a person to understand the most profound utterances about the mystery if the Mystery itself languishes unloved?

In one of his sermons (which I can no longer trace), St. Augustine asks the congregation, "Do you believe?" They answer, "Yes, we believe!" He tells them: "Then live your faith and you have true faith."

I used to think that this meant that I should make my life conform to the tenets of my faith. If I believe in life everlasting, I should not make this earth a permanent abode; if I believe that God was enfleshed, then I should respect, even revere all flesh and cherish this world sanctified by His presence; and so forth. But then, one day, I came to realize that there was another meaning to St. Augustine's injunction. If to believe is to establish contact, then to live one's faith is to be enlivened by that immeasurable source of life. Faith is like a switch between the little motor that runs my life and the Dynamo from whom all power comes. To turn on the switch is to be turned on, to be set in motion in the world. It is this realization that prompted St. Paul to exclaim, "The life I now live is not my life, but the life which Christ lives in me."[35]

Living my faith, then, means paramountly to let the divine energy flow through me. The details are secondary; the important thing is to be the conduit through which the water Source tapped by faith flows freely into the world.

When the Whirling Dervishes dance in their prayer hall, they hold their right hands open, palm up, and their left hands open, palm down. The symbolism is this: as they commune with God they become the channels through which God's grace is scattered over the world.[36]

FAITH AND THE INEFFABLE

What does it mean to confront the ineffable in faith? Al-Hallāj says that the Prophet Mohammed "blinked beyond the where," implying that the ineffable is beyond space and time, and the Bible says that when Elijah desired to see God, a great wind swept the mountain shattering rocks in its path, but God was not in the wind; then an earthquake shook the mountain, but God was not in the earthquake; then a fire raged through the mountain's side, but God was not in the fire; finally there was the sound of sheer silence, and Elijah knew he was in the presence of God.[37] Similarly, when Arjuna beheld the divine Lord Krishna in His supreme form, "His face facing everywhere," resplendent as if the light of a thousand suns were ablaze in the sky, he was struck with such amazement that his hair stood on end and he fell prostrate on the ground with hands and feet folded in respect.[38]

Here I am trying to emphasize the subjective part of the experience, what it feels like to be open toward the mystery, the beyond, whatever the name we give it. Otto speaks of a sense of "absolute unapproachability," a feeling of being utterly overpowered by the forbidding majesty of Being, or of God,[39] and this characterization seems to come close to the experience. But these feelings are not always present in faith, and certainly do not mark the length and breadth of it. Rather, they arise occasionally, perhaps at crucial moments in the life of the believer, and they leave an after taste that can be savored again even after many years.[40]

My point here is that the openness to the beyond that characterizes faith is not a purely cognitive state but carries with it extraordinary feelings, and this whether the beyond is conceived as having the reality of God, of Being, or simply as possessing the quality of infinitude that overwhelms us when contemplating the limitless horizon — something that must have touched the soul of the psalmist when he sang,

> When I see your heavens,
> the work of your fingers,
> the moon and the stars which you created,
> I ask,
> "What are we that you should think of us,
> what are we humans that you should care for us?"[41]

CONCLUSION

I have set parts of this chapter in terms of my own personal development, but this is not fortuitous. James Fowler has shown recently that faith does, in fact, develop and that it goes through stages corresponding, broadly, to the stages of development described by Piaget, Erikson, and Kohlberg.

I do not pretend to have reached Stage 6, Universalizing Faith, as described by Fowler. At any rate, Fowler says this stage is "exceedingly rare,"[42] and the examples he gives involve Mahatma Gandhi, Dietrich Bonhoeffer, Abraham Heschel, Thomas Merton, Houston Smith, Simone Weil, and similar ones. The point I have been trying to convey is that ultimately, faith, when it has been allowed to bloom and when it has been cultivated with care, goes beyond the strictures of dogmas and becomes an openness to the Infinite. Developmentally it takes years to get there. My point is that this *is* what faith really is.

NOTES

1. Thus, Walter Kaufmann, in *Critique of Religion and Philosophy* (New York: Anchor Books, 1961), § 36, p. 112, wrote, "I believe that something is true if, and only if, I think it is true. . . . When I am asked whether I really believe something . . . I am asked whether I am in earnest." The reason why I say "I think it is true," is "the lack of evidence sufficient to compel the assent of every reasonable person" (p. 113). See also his *The Faith of a Heretic* (New York: Anchor Books, 1963), pp. 2-3.

2. Israel Scheffler, *Conditions of Knowledge* (Chicago: Scott, Foresman & Co., 1965); Paul Tillich, *Dynamics of Faith* (New York: Harper Torchbooks, 1958); Louis Jacobs, *Faith* (New York: Basic Books, 1968).

3. Jacobs, *Faith*, Chapter 1; Scheffler, *Conditions of Knowledge*, pp. 14-18.

4. Timothy D. Barnes, *Tertullian. A Historical and Literary Study* (Oxford: Oxford University Press, 1971), p. 224.

5. See V. Décarie, "Le paradoxe de Tertullien," *Vigiliae Christianae* 15 (1961), p. 23 *ff.*

6. B.A.O. Williams, "Tertullian's Paradox," in *New Essays in Philosophical Theology*, A. N. Flew and A. MacIntyre, eds. (New York: Macmillan, 1966). Also Alfred Jules Ayer, *Language, Truth and Logic* (New York: Dover Publications, Inc., n.d.), p. 118.

7. Tertullian, *Adversus Marc.* IV, 10, 6-7. *Tertulliani Opera. Corpus Christianorum, series latina* (Turnhout: Brepols, 1954). Also: "Since he is born of man, being the Son of Man, he has a body derived from a body. You may, I assure you, more easily find a man born without a heart or without brains . . . than without a body" (*Adversus Marc.* IV, 10, 16). Hans Jonas, *Gnosticism* (Boston: Beacon Press, 1963), pp. 137, 146.

8. *Adversus Marc.* V, 19, 8.

9. *De Carne Christi* 3, 1.

10. *De Carne Christi* 5.

11. Thus Williams, "Tertullian's Paradox," p. 211.

12. Henry Chadwick, *Early Christian Thought and the Classical Tradition* (New York: Oxford University Press, 1966), p. 1 *ff.* grants Tertullian's uniqueness in this regard, though I think he disarms the paradox.

13. William James, "The Will to Believe," in *Essays in Pragmatism* (New York: Hafner Publishing Co., 1966), p. 88.

14. Ibid., pp. 95 and 101.

15. Ibid., pp. 94-95.

16. Blaise Pascal, *Pensées* #282 (New York: E. P. Dutton & Co., 1958), p. 79.

17. St. Augustine, *De praedestinatione sanctorum* 2, 5; ML 44, 962.

18. William James, *The Principles of Psychology*, Chapter 21, "Relations of Belief and Will," in *Great Books of the Western World*, Robert M. Hutchins, ed. (Chicago: Encyclopaedia Britannica, 1952), Vol. 53, p. 661.

19. "Pathological" in its etymological meaning, from *pathein*, to experience or undergo. Søren Kierkegaard, *The Journals* (Oxford: Oxford University Press, 1938), No. 1044.

20. Søren Kierkegaard, *Concluding Unscientific Postscript* (Princeton, NJ: Princeton University Press, 1968), p. 540.

21. Ibid., p. 504.

22. Kierkegaard, *The Journals*, No. 922. Also his *Philosophical Fragments* (Princeton, NJ: Princeton University Press, 1962), IV, p. 73.

23. *Philosophical Fragments*, p. 46.

24. Lawrence Ferlinghetti, *A Coney Island of the Mind* (New York: New Directions, 1958), No. 15, p. 30.

25. St. Augustine, *De agone christiano* 13, 14; ML 40, 299.

26. Tillich, *Dynamics of Faith*, p. 8.

27. Henri de Lubac, S. J., *Catholicism* (New York: Mentor-Omega, 1964), p.182.

28. Daisetz T. Suzuki, *The Essentials of Zen Buddhism* (London: Rider & Co., 1962), p. 307.

29. St. Augustine, *Confessions* I, 1. See Rudolf Otto, *The Idea of the Holy* (New York: Oxford University Press, 1958).

30. "What does it mean to believe in Him? It means, in faith, to love, to cherish, and to go in to Him and be made one with him" (St. Augustine, *In Ioannis Evangel.*, tract. 29, 6 [ML 35, 1651]).

31. Karl Barth, *The Epistle to the Romans* (London: Oxford University Press, 1933), I, 16, p. 39.

32. *Contra* St. Anselm, *Proslogium*, Ch. I: "I believe in order to understand; for this also I believe, that unless I believe, I shall not understand."   St. Anselm, *Proslogium; Monologium; An Appendix on Behalf of the Fool by Gaunilon; and Cur Deus Homo*, Sidney Norton Dean, transl. (Chicago: The Open Court Publishing Co., 1933). The same idea in St. Augustine's *In Ioannis Evangel.*, tract. 29, 6; ML 35, 1630. See also Karl Barth, *Fides quaerens intellectum: Anselms Bewis der Existenz Gottes* (Munich: Kaiser Verlag, 1931).

33. This marvelous story by Apuleius contains many levels of meaning, one which, surely, reflects the ancient belief that no mortal could see God and live. This was the answer YHWH gave to Moses (*Exodus* 33:20) and to Elijah (*I Kings* 19:10-13), and Krishna gave Arjuna (*Bhagavadgītā* XI). Psyche did eventually see Eros, and she was severely punished as a result, though she did not die, perhaps because she only saw the mortal shape of her immortal lover.

34. Abraham Heschel, *Israel: An Echo of God* (New York: Farrar, Straus & Giroux, 1969), p. 224.

35. *Galatians* 2:20.

36. Eva de Vitray-Meyerovitch, *Rūmī and Sufism* (Sausalito, CA: The Post-Apollo Press, 1987), pp. 43-53.

37. *I Kings* 19:11-12.

38. *Bhagavadgītā* 11:9-14.

39. Otto, *The Idea of the Holy*, pp. 19-20.

40. The feeling of presence gives rise to many issues of an epistemological and theological nature, issues of importance which cannot be tackled here. See Josef Maréchal, S. J., *Studies in the Psychology of the Mystics* (Albany, NY: Magi Books, Inc., 1964); William James, *The Varieties of Religious Experience* (New York: Mentor, 1964); Robert K. C. Forman, ed., *The Problem of Pure Consciousness* (New York: Oxford University Press, 1990).

41. *Psalm* 8:4-5.

42. James W. Fowler, *Stages of Faith* (San Francisco: Harper & Row, 1981), p. 200.

3

Faith and Paradox: Cases

Faith and paradox share the same structure. Faith is paradoxical. Besides the theoretical understanding of this identity, we need to explore in some detail how the paradoxical nature of faith plays itself out in the actual lives of people — even legendary people. This is the task of the present chapter.

ABRAHAM AS THE KNIGHT OF FAITH

Kierkegaard makes a distinction between the tragic hero and the believer, whom he calls "the knight of faith." Agamemnon is a tragic hero. When the allied fleet carrying the warriors to Troy is stranded for lack of favorable winds and the cause of this obstacle is traced to him, he sacrifices his daughter Iphigenia.[1] He gives up his duty to her for the sake of his duty to his army. He does not set his own particular duty toward his daughter over his universal duty to all as commander-in-chief. Therefore he is justified, in a way, by fulfilling the universal duty to the majority over his own. On the other hand, the believer acts only out of an absolute individual duty toward God which cannot be generalized or justified ethically. The tragic hero is justified by the universal; the believer only in himself;[2] that is, as individual. Here, then, is the paradox, that the individual believer sets himself or herself above the universal, the ethical; that belief sets itself above universal ethics.[3] This is the case with Abraham.

We do not know, of course, what God Abraham worshiped: the Bible story was written at least a thousand years after he lived and by people who were intent in establishing a line of belief back to the origin of their people, a succession of believers in the same God as they *then* believed in. They did not have in mind a concern for accuracy and historical truth: they merely wanted to prove their point, that their origins were noble and ancient, and that this God they now worshiped had been the God of their ancestors all the way back to Ur of the Chaldeans, as unhistorical and unpsychological as this would have been; for we worship the gods of the people among whom we are born, and the gods of the people of Ur were the Moon God Nanna and his consort, the Moon Goddess Ningal, and not the God of Israel, which did not exist. And yet the story of Abraham as he prepared to sacrifice his son Isaac is valid, for it is the story of a man confronting his own obscurity and the paradox of his faith. He may not have gone out of the land of his ancestors by faith, as the pseudo-Pauline *Letter to the Hebrews* claimed; he may not have dwelled among strangers in a strange land by faith; but it was by faith that he rose in the middle of the night, after a dream, determined to confront the paradox.

We need not suppose, as the Bible does, that God tempted Abraham. It is enough to assume that he felt compelled to entertain seriously the paradox of a God who granted him a child and then demanded that he sacrifice the child to him. It is enough to assume that he would have challenged himself to see if his faith was strong enough to deal with the paradox. For calling the incident a temptation or a test does not diminish the paradox: whoever believes in a good god who demands an evil action is confronted by the paradox as long as he understands what it means for a god to be good and for the sacrifice of a human life to be evil. For there have been religions in which human sacrifices were routinely demanded by the gods so that the sacrifice of one's child would have been a meritorious act; but for a good god, a god of life, such as is assumed here, to demand an evil deed, a deed of death, is a paradox no matter what exculpatory title one give to it.

And Abraham believed that it was God who tempted him. This is part of the paradox. Sartre asks, "How did he know it was really God?" A woman, says Sartre, used to receive phone calls from God. How did she know it was God at the other end of the line? "He says it's God," she replied.[4] And the "Son of Sam," in New York City, heard the voice of God commanding him to shoot down unsuspecting lovers in his neighborhood: how did he know it was God? But Abraham knew, or he thought he knew; he was sure it was God, and this is essential to the paradox. So Abraham believed, as Kierkegaard says, and did not doubt; "he believed in the preposterous,"[5] and he did so because this is the way of faith, this is what it means to believe. Warm feelings in the breast and languorous, tear-filled eyes raised to heaven is not faith; recital of ardent prayers is not faith; proclamations of belief are not faith. Faith is the paradox, belief in the preposterous.

Ethically and legally we would call Abraham a would-be murderer; religiously we might say that his act, the intended sacrifice of his son Isaac, was an act of faith. The contradiction between the two, when confronted existentially and not merely in theory, is the paradox, and is the origin of the anguish (*Angst*) of Abraham. Preachers and commentators who wax eloquent about Abraham usually forget this anguish, and therefore their preaching is ineffectual; for without the anguish of the paradox, Abraham's act is unimportant.[6] In fact, without the paradox of faith there is nothing to imitate in Abraham, for his intended act was murder. But his absolute allegiance to the will of God which caused him to find his duty in what ethics would ordinarily forbid, this is what is to be imitated even though the reward is the insurmountable anguish of faith[7] and the frustrating inability of not being able to make oneself understood by others.[8] The significance of Abraham's life lies in the paradox of faith.[9]

I should add that Kierkegaard's interpretation of Abraham's act is brilliant but, in a way, flawed, because Abraham's behavior meets all the criteria of a fanatical act (as we shall see). Fanatics believe absolutely, even if the exercise of their beliefs leads them to subordinate other people's interests to their own. Typically, fanatics are so sure of themselves that they would rather die than switch. By individualizing Abraham's case Kierkegaard manages to avoid the accusation of fanaticism, but not everybody would accept this subterfuge.

A similar argument is often made with regard to the hero, in whose case death is endured, also, beyond the ethical precept of self-preservation. In both cases, there is a primacy of the will over reason, so that the believer and the hero act, as it were, beyond the logical. Emerson put it well:

> There is somewhat non philosophical in heroism; there is somewhat not holy in it. . . . Heroism feels and never reasons, and therefore is always right; and although a different breeding, different religion, and greater intellectual activity would have modified or even reversed the particular action, yet for the hero that thing he does is the highest deed, and is not open to the censure of philosophers or divines.[10]

SATAN AS TRAGIC LOVER

The notion of rebellion is one that is rooted in the human consciousness and experience. As an idea, it is immensely old. It appears in Sumeria in the person of Gilgamesh, who refuses Ishtar's advances, and then in the Bible, where Lilith, the woman created at the same time as Adam, refused to be "under him," and eventually walked out on him, an action that necessitated the creation of a tamer model.[11] It appears in Job, too, who, tired of suffering and of being wrongly blamed for his misfortunes, queries God, who never directly answers him. It appears in Prometheus, the Titan who opposes Zeus's insensitivity toward the human race and who steadfastly refuses to disclose to the Ruler of the gods the secret of his future undoing. It appears in the figure of Antigone, the young woman who challenges the powers of the state in the name of brotherly love; and, of course, it appears in Lucifer, who, legend says, refused to obey his Creator and was therefore hurled from heaven to hell to be forever our woeful bane.

These and many other figures of the rebel, ancient as well as modern, Eastern and Western, have been studied in depth,[12] and I do not presume to have something new and unusual to say about them. My goal is more modest. I would like to expose a facet, as it were, a twist, a wrinkle in the story of Lucifer — or Satan, as he is more commonly known. It is an angle that appears, I believe, only in Muslim Sufi literature, in the writings of a great, though controversial, Muslim mystic, Al-Husayn ibn Mansūr al-Hallāj. His picture of Satan as a tragic lover is so unique and yet inspiring that I believe it deserves to be considered in some detail. It is also an example of how the paradox of faith may be confronted.

In what follows I will first present briefly the traditional story of the Fall of the angels and then expound on the vision of al-Hallāj.

Theological Speculation

Christian theologians generally speculate that the angels, created originally good and holy, suffered attrition in their ranks, so that some of them became evil. The *fact* of their fall is grounded on a text from *2 Peter* 2:4, "God did not spare the angels who sinned, but consigned them to the dark pits of hell." Strictly speaking, the nature of this prevarication is unknown, as no scripture clearly identifies it,[13] but that their malice is due to their own choice or choices is clear, for, as *Genesis* says, God created only good beings and therefore would have created all of them good.[14]

The Patristic tradition asserts that the number of sinful angels was large and that their "sin" was either carnal desire (for which a weak argument is *Genesis* 6:2 *ff.*) or overweening pride, since all sin is rooted in some form of self-exaltation.[15] As Augustine put it, "they turned away from the Supreme to themselves, who were not supreme."[16] The common doctrine holds that the sin consisted in wanting "to be like God,"[17] for, according to Aquinas, to aspire to achieve salvation by one's powers alone is to desire what belongs only to God to grant, and is, therefore, a case of extreme pride.[18]

Some think, however, that the sin of the angels was more specific. As Delbanco puts it, "According to Justin Martyr and Irenaeus, the fall of Satan followed the creation of man and was occasioned by his festering jealousy of Adam as a rival in the affections of God."[19] The story claims that God commanded the angels to "worship" Adam but that Lucifer refused and was therefore punished. This story appears in an old "*Vita Adae et Evae*" probably dating from the first century C.E.[20] Following this tradition, Augustine, for example, says that Satan fell "because he envied the fact that humans had been created in God's image."[21] Others, however, following Lactantius (*ca.* 260-340), contended that in the very divine act that created the angels, God manifested to them His plan of redeeming fallen humanity (which had not been created yet!) through the incarnation, death, and resurrection of Christ. God revealed to the angels that their service to Him would eventually entail service to the Word incarnate, a plan some of the angels rejected as implying submission to a being they deemed inferior to themselves.[22] Hence the animosity of the fallen angels against humanity; that is, against those whose future salvation required the incarnation, which in turn triggered their own rebellion. Since the Fall, they would appear to be bent on thwarting the execution of the salvific plan they had rejected in the first place. This is the origin of the theme, common in many orthodox as well as Gnostic sources, of preventing the fallen angels from knowing the time and manner of the incarnation lest they conspire to impede it.

At a different level of speculation, Paul Tillich contends that the story of the Fall of the angels is a mythological way of expressing the transition from essence to existence, from dream to reality, and this, indeed, is the form in which the legend first appears in Judaeo-Christian literature.[23] For the idea of "Fall" implies a sudden and dramatic transition from a privileged state, such as that of being a possibility in God's essence, to the precarious state of existing as quasi-independent realities in the world. For example, when fiction writers set down their imagined characters to a page, they cannot predict with certainty the life these characters will demand as the story develops in detail. The move from imagination to reality is fraught with danger. This, in a grand and cosmic scale, is, according to Tillich, what the myth of the Fall of the angels describes.

In Christianity, the scriptural origins of the myth of the angelic fall are somewhat obscure. The Gospel of Luke quotes a *logion* of Jesus to his followers after their return from a preaching mission. Full of themselves and astonished at their powers, they told Jesus that even the spirits (δαιμόνια) obeyed them. Jesus, wanting to warn them about pride, said to them, "I have often watched Satan fall like lighting from heaven."[24] And he added, to make his meaning clear: "Do not rejoice at the fact that spirits obey you, but, rather, that your names are written in heaven."[25] The contrast, here, is between the fact that the disciples' names are written in heaven and that Satan has fallen from heaven, and the implication is that anyone, even Satan, can fall, even from heaven.[26]

The mention of Satan, the tempter who appears in postexilic literature (probably under the influence of Persian dualism) as a member of God's court bent on testing pious and upright people, and the image of his Fall from heaven, associated this Lucan passage with Isaiah's vision of the fall of the King of Babylon in *Isaiah* 14: 12, "How have you fallen from heaven, O Shining One, son of the Dawn!" The Day Star, "Shining One," (Gr. *phosphoros*; Hebr. *heylel*; Lat. *lucifer*, "bearer of light"), was the planet Venus as Morning Star. This appellation was given also to several goddesses, like Inanna, Artemis, Aurora, and Hecate. However, at some point, in the case at hand, it was anthropomorphized and tied to Satan, so that the two became synonymous. That Jesus had actually "seen" Satan-Lucifer fall from the heavens to hell became a "proof" that he had existed eternally and would have been present at the creation of all the angels; but for the purposes of this book, the important thing is the association of the pride of the King of Babylon (probably Tiglath-Pilneser, *ca.* 716 B.C.E.) with an assumed pride in Lucifer, a pride that caused him to fall from heaven — in fact, to be thrown out and down, as *Revelation* 12:9 has it.[27]

The Dante Connection

In his *Commedia*, Dante alluded to the tradition that made Lucifer a fallen angel now enthroned as King of Hell. In *Inferno*, Canto 34, Dante borrows the opening line of the sacred hymn of Venantius Fortunatus († *ca.* 600), *Vexilla Regis* [*coeli*], and applies it to Lucifer:

> " '*Vexilla regis prodeunt inferni*'
> verso di noi; però dimanzi mira"
> disse'l maestro mio, "se tu discerni."

> "'The banners of the King of Hell' advance
> toward us; look well,"
> my Master said, "if you can spot him."

Surrounded by awful shades, Dante cowers behind Virgil until Virgil steps aside and points Satan to him: "Ecco Dite!"[28] "Behold the Lord!" he says — *Dis*, Hades, god of the underworld, a most terrifying divinity for the ancients, whose proper name was not to be invoked.

Here the initial royalty of Lucifer is acknowledged through the association with Venantius's hymn, and the fallen nature, too, is explicitly portrayed in the frightful vision of the poet.[29]

Milton's Lost Paradise

But perhaps the most complete rendering of the Lucifer myth is that of Milton in *Paradise Lost*. Book V describes the divine decree by which the Almighty anointed his only begotten Son and placed him above all creatures:

> your Head I him appoint;
> And by my Self have sworn to him shall bow
> All knees in Heav'n, and shall confess him Lord.[30]

Whoever shall disobey him will be deemed to disobey the Almighty, and such action will be judged to break the universal union of all, and it will bring as consequence being cast out from God and plunged to utter darkness without the possibility of redemption, without end. Satan, however,

> . . . . fraught
> With envie against the Son of God . . . could not beare
> Through pride that sight, and thought himself impaird.[31]

We have here the essential lines of the story told so far, but Milton gives as cause of the revolt, not just envy of Adam, but the wounded pride of Lucifer refusing to acknowledge Christ as equal to God. Book VI contains the lengthy description of the battle between Michael's army and Satan's hordes, ending with the latter's defeat and confinement to hell. Adam is then warned that Satan now envies his state and plots to seduce him in order to make him share his own eternal punishment in hell.[32] Hence the legend, as Chesterton put it, "that all evil began with some attempt at superiority; some moment when, as we might say, the very skies were cracked across like a mirror because there was a sneer in heaven."[33]

Satan in the *Qur'ān*

The *Qur'ān* preserves the story of the prevarication of Satan in essentially the same traditional form, except that there is no mention of Christ, much less a refusal to acknowledge him. The question of submission is to Adam only. Several passages retell the event; for example:

> Then We said to the angels: "Prostrate yourselves before Adam." They all prostrated themselves except Satan, who refused to prostrate himself.
> "Why did you not prostrate yourself when I commanded you?" He asked.
> "I am nobler than he," he replied. "You created me from fire, but You created him from clay."
> He said: "Get you down hence! This is no place for your contemptuous pride. Away with you!"[34]

The elements of the story involve the comparison with Adam, the refusal *because of pride*, and the ensuing enmity between Satan and Adam and his descendants.[35] Human temptation is Satan's revenge. As is to be expected, no mention is made of Christ. However, in the *Qur'ān* and elsewhere, Satan (*al-*

Shaytān, "the adversary") is given a personal name, Iblīs ('Azāzīl or Hārith before his fall, as in *Leviticus* 16:20), which is an abbreviation of the Greek *diabolos*, "slanderer." Rūmī sings:

> See in everyone's face a wondrous moon.
> > When you have seen the beginning, see the end
> So that you do not become like Iblīs, one-eyed.
> > Half he sees, half not, like some defective.
> He saw Adam's clay, but his faith he saw not;
> > He saw the world in him, but his other-worldly eye he saw not.[36]

What Iblīs supposedly does not see is the new spiritual nature of Adam which "links him to God in an intimacy never before permitted to creatures."[37] This Adamic characteristic is the foundation of the mystical union. The failure to see it is due to Iblīs's lack of faith.

According to the commentators, Iblīs's cry, "I am better than he!"[38] is a revelation of pride. In Rūmī's words, "The calamity of Iblīs was his 'I am the better one!' "[39] However, *Qur'ān* 66:6 says that angels do not disobey, and therefore a legend was woven around Iblīs that he was originally born a *jinn* but was raised as an angel, his natural rebellious nature coming to light when God commanded him to worship Adam. Others, however, counter that if Iblīs had not been a true angel he would not have been asked to worship Adam.

Two main reasons are given for the refusal: that Adam is "younger" than Iblīs, and that he was made of clay while Iblīs was made of fire. But underlying both, as Rūmī claimed, is Iblīs's lack of faith. Iblīs's final condemnation is delayed until the Day of Resurrection and Judgment, a point elaborated by Tewfik El Hakim in his short story, "The Martyr."[40] In the story, Gabriel replies to Iblīs's request for forgiveness, "You are too early. This is not the time to change the established order. . . . The order of creation may not be upset by mercy and forgiveness."[41] The Muslim's bow in prayer is a reminder of what happens when one refuses to bow, as Iblīs did.[42]

Unlike its Christian counterpart, which dwells only on Satan's pride and disobedience, early Sufi speculation in Islam dwells on the paradox that this case presents — like finding a sign warning, "Don't get wet!" under a cataract. As 'Ain Al-Qudāt put it,

> He cast him into the ocean, firmly bound, and said to him,
> "You there! Take care not to get wet!"[43]

One way of stating this paradox is by means of a difference noted between God's *will* (*irāda*) and God's *command* (*amr*). Awn states the paradox succinctly: "How does one obey a [divine]command that contradicts the will of God?"[44] Sufis consider this confrontation between will and command to be the crucial paradox of Iblīs, his personal tragedy. What is the paradox? That he sets himself above the universal ethic of obedience to God's command because of his allegiance to God's will. God's command justifies the obedient behavior of all the other angels; his allegiance to God's will justifies only him. Iblīs was the first one to experience this paradox. Part of the problem is that God's command is more clearly discernible than his will. That's why, as we shall see, Iblīs is able to "blame" God's will — use God's will as justification — and claim that he is following, truly, God's will even while disobeying God's command.

From another point of view, the paradox results from the absolute unicity of God; for given this oneness, there should be no room for divergence of opinion or disobedience, no room for the worship of another. To illustrate this, a story is told of al-Junayd (died 297/910) that at one point in his life he came face to face with Iblīs. Overwhelmed with horror at the sight, he still managed to ask: "Why would you not bow down to Adam, for which God cursed you?" "Junayd," responded Iblīs, "how could you imagine that I should bow down to any except God?"

Startled by this reply, unlike any in the extant literature, Junayd sensed a trick in the answer, a desperate effort at self-justification, and mumbled to himself, "You're lying — if you had been an obedient servant you would not have disobeyed his command." Iblīs overheard him and exclaimed, "O God! You've burnt me!" and vanished suddenly,[45] acknowledging, by his disappearance, that this had not been the real reason for his disobedience. In other words, Junayd dismisses Iblīs's paradoxical answer as a false pretext for refusing obedience, but in doing so he overlooks the paradox.

This story of Junayd's comes close to the meaning we shall find in al-Hallāj; but whereas Junayd takes Iblīs's explanation as a lie, as an effort to exculpate himself, al-Hallāj takes it seriously, perhaps because he understands in a profound sense the dilemma created by God's command, and is not willing to wriggle out of it. It is as if only al-Hallāj were willing to give the devil his due.

Actually, al-Hallāj is not alone in his appraisal. Three hundred years after his death, Ibn Ghānim Al-Maqdisī, in his *Taflīs Iblīs*, describes Iblīs's explanation in words reminiscent of those of al-Hallāj; and 'Attār, in *Tadhkirat al-awliyā'*, calls Iblīs "the sacrificed one of God." Ahmed Ghazālī, too, writes that "when Iblīs was driven away, he did not diminish his service, nor his love, nor his *dhikr* in the least way."[46] Acknowledging the disobedience and even deeming it reprehensible, the Sufis still see Iblīs as an example of the paradox of faith and of the confrontation between will (*irāda*) and command (*amr*). Iblīs, says Awn, is the "spiritual model for all Muslims because he, more perfectly than any other being, witnessed to the Unity and Oneness of God, even at the expense of self-destruction."[47] Similarly, El Hakim has Iblīs claim, "Here I stand with unequaled and unsurpassed love for Thee. . . . A love that requires a sacrifice hitherto unknown."[48] This is the reason why Iblīs concludes, "I am a martyr — I am a martyr."[49]

Iblīs as Tragic Lover

Let me turn now to al-Hallāj's interpretation of the refusal. Al-Hallāj (died 309/922) was a disciple of Junayd, though the latter is said to have been wary of the unorthodoxy of his pupil's views. If al-Sarrāj (died 378/988) is accurate in his narrative about Junayd's encounter with Iblīs, Hallāj must have heard the same story, and it may have influenced his own unique and unparalleled retelling of the angelic fall.

In a remarkable work, the *TāSīn of before-time and ambiguity*, al-Hallāj draws a picture of Iblīs at once profound and paradoxical. Its various sections sustain an argument that renders the figure of Iblīs into a loyal lover willing to endure rejection by God and separation from him even unto hell, rather than betray his love for God and his acknowledgment of God's supremacy.

> He [Iblīs] was told: "Bow down!" He said, "[to] no other!" He was asked, "Even if you receive my curse?" He said, "It does not matter. I have no way to an other-than-you. I am an abject lover."[50]

The reason given for the refusal to acknowledge Adam is that Iblīs's whole being is focused on God to the exclusion of all other beings, as the *Qur'ān* requires: "Say: 'God is One, the Eternal God. He begot none, nor was He begotten. None is equal to Him.' "[51] This is the source of the *shahādah*, "There is no god but God," an affirmation which dwells in the heart and on the mouth of every believer.

The tradition, however, claims that Iblīs grew proud. To this charge of pride, according to al-Hallāj, Iblīs replied:

> "A moment with you would be enough to justify my pride . . . so much more am I justified when I have passed the ages with you."[52]

This profound justification of his refusal and, even, of his pride, is followed by another that hinges on predestination: God has predestined him *ab aeterno* so that his actions are all in God's hands: "To you belongs the determination and the choice," he says. There follows a mystical poem of extraordinary beauty. Iblīs sings:

> There can be no distance for me
> Distancing you from me
> When I have achieved certainty
> Nearness and distance are one.
> Even if I am abandoned
> Abandonment will be my companion.
> How can it be abandonment
> While love is one?
> To you, praise in success,
> In the pure absolute
> For a servant of true heart
> Who will bow to no other than you.[53]

With sure insight al-Hallāj understands that union and separation are the paradoxical conditions of the mystical life, for Iblīs and for everyone else, for "unless one has previously experienced union, one cannot know separation."[54]

Iblīs then explains that God's injunction to bow to Adam was not really a command but a test of his love and commitment to God, which remain as strong in exile as they were before: "Knowing remains as sound as it was before, unchanged; only the figure has been transformed"[55] — that is, the locale and the outward circumstances. As a result, says Iblīs, his service is now purer, his remembrance of God stronger and more focused.[56] The following passage describes the paradoxical situation in which Iblīs now finds himself:

> He set me apart, "extased me" when he expelled me, so that I would not be mixed with the pure-hearted. He held me back from others because of my zeal, othered me because of my bewilderment, bewildered me because of my exile, exiled me because of my service, proscribed me because of my friendship, disfigured me because of my praise, consecrated me because of my *hijra*, abandoned me because of my unveiling, unveiled me because of my union, made me one with him because of my separation, cut me off because of the preclusion of my fate.[57]

According to Awn,

> The curse inflicted on Iblīs is not a gesture of divine aggression; it is a challenge to Iblīs and a test of the quality of his love. God's act demands a response; the crux is whether the response will be the resentful cries of the self-styled victim who bemoans having been singled out as the object of divine persecution, or the expressions of magnanimous love from the grateful servant who accepts God's gift of pain because it comes from His hand.[58]

Iblīs concludes:

> Even if he torments me with his fire forever and beyond, I will not bow before any other than him, abase myself before a figure and body, or recognize a rival or offspring. My proclamation is the proclamation of those who are sincere, and in love I am triumphant. How not?[59]

Comments and Conclusions

There is nothing like al-Hallāj's meditation in the traditional Christian literature. The Fall of Lucifer is accepted literally as a refusal to serve (*"Non serviam!"*) and the consequences are recounted in great detail. Once this revolt is in progress, there is no compunction in Satan, no effort at reconciliation. Pride takes over and completely overshadows his prior splendor. Pride it is, says Milton, that "cast him out from Heav'n, with all his Host."[60] Rather than entertain regret, Satan comments, "Better to reign in Hell, then serve in Heav'n,"[61] thus emphasizing once again the tradition of rebellion.

There is a parallel to this case in the story of Abraham and Isaac.[62] Most commentators and preachers are satisfied dealing with this story at the superficial level of a mere temptation: Abraham's faith is tested and he comes through with flying colors. Only Kierkegaard accords the story the fullness of paradox, the paradox of faith — "a paradox which is capable of transforming a murder into a holy act well-pleasing to God, a paradox which gives Isaac back to Abraham, *which no thought can master, because faith begins precisely there where thinking leaves off*."[63] This kind of existential insight is lacking in the case of Satan in its Christian garb.

At the theoretical level, according to Aquinas, it would have been possible for Satan to experience sorrow, since sorrow is a concomitant of the sense of loss;[64] but there is no mystical contemplation of this loss nor of the conditions of it.[65] It is taken for granted that the command involves no difficulty. The tendency has been to aggrandize the evil of the devil's pride and the extent of his desire for revenge, which eventuates in the many temptations with which he makes human life precarious.

Through the Middle Ages, especially, Satan acquired an almost independent existence, a reality of frightful proportions, manifested often in possessions, principally of women, as in the case of witchcraft. Christians everywhere acted as though Satan had a power equal to God's, a power he used continually to thwart God's plans. This Manichaean view was not official, of course, but it was common, partly because the prevalence of evil in life and in society demanded some sort of personification of it so as to have a focus to rail against. This idolization has greatly subsided, but it may have prevented, while it lasted, any mystical, or even mythical, approach to Satan. Today possession has become obsession, malice is explainable by reference to upbringing or deprivation, cataclysms are natural phenomena, and Satan himself can at times be a friendly figure as in the case of Faust and in Douglass Wallop's delightful novel, *The Year the Yankees Lost the Pennant* (1954). All evil, for the most part, being explainable, there is no need of Satan.

Against this background, the case of al-Hallāj's Iblīs stands out even more starkly. We thrive on stories of doomed lovers, and here is one whose love surpassed all manner of affection even when his action made him the lowest of rejects. The Christian interpretation hinges on the omnipotence of God and Lucifer's disobedience; al-Hallāj's, on the other hand, takes cognizance of the paradox created by the divine command: to obey or love one other than God is a betrayal of God's omnipotence and unicity, while not to obey is an equal betrayal. One is doomed if one does and is doomed if one doesn't. The Miltonian interpretation, following Lactantius, gets around this by making Jesus divine, but only barely; when the command involves only Adam, the paradox blossoms in full force.

We do not know exactly when al-Hallāj penned — or dictated — his little mystical meditation. At some point, however, he found himself in a position similar to that of Iblīs. His paradoxical insistence that he was so oned with God that he could claim, "I am the real" (*anâ l-haqq*),[66] or, as another version would have it, "I am he whom I love, he whom I love is I," brought him to his death, as Junayd had feared: he was flogged, mutilated, and exposed on the gibbet. Even though the reasons for his execution were more complex than I have intimated here, there is a certain irony to the fact that his Iblīs was as much a tragic lover as he became.[67]

CONCLUSION

There is a sixteenth century poem popularly attributed to Saint Teresa of Ávila (1515-1582) but generally considered anonymous. It reads like this:

> 'Tis not the heaven Thou hast promised me
> that moves me, dear Lord, to so love Thee,
> and 'tis no threat of hell, how terrible it be,
> that keeps me from offending Thee.

> Thou movest me, my Lord; it doth move me
> to see Thee crucified and taunted by the mob;
> to see Thy body wounded doth move me;
> Thy death and Thy affronts move me to sob.
>
> Last, I am so moved, Lord, by Thy love,
> that though there were no heaven I would love Thee,
> and though there were no hell I would fear Thee.
>
> For this my love, Lord, Thou must not pay me,
> for even if I hoped naught from above,
> so would, as now, for e'er remain my love.[68]

The same sentiments appear in a story about Rabi'a, the saintly woman of Basra (died 801), narrated by Aflākī:

> One day some friends-of-God saw Rabi'a running along with fire in one hand and water in the other. "Lady of the next world, where are you going and what does this mean?"
> Rabi'a replied: "I am going to burn paradise and douse hell-fire, so that both veils may be lifted from those on the quest and they will become sincere of purpose. God's servants will learn to see him without hope for reward or fear of punishment. As it is now, if you took away hope for reward or fear of punishment, no one would worship or obey."[69]

A similar story is narrated by 'Attār in *Tadhikrat al-'Awliyā'* (Memorial of the Friends of God) and repeated in the form of a prayer, as follows:

> "O Lord, if I worship you out of fear of hell, burn me in hell. If I worship you in the hope of paradise, forbid it to me. And if I worship you for your own sake, do not deprive me of your eternal beauty."[70]

One major point of the stories is the inadequacy of dogmas and teachings when it comes to the love of God. In fact, the stories contain a warning against putting too much stock in such beliefs, for they distract from the true approach to God. They seem to convey the idea that true faith opens itself totally to the Divine without the need of threats, promises of rewards, and dogmatic pronouncements. I believe these stories stand out as confirmation of the major points developed in this chapter.

NOTES

1. At least in one version of the story. In another, like another Isaac, she is spared in the nick of time by Ariadne, who transports her safely to Aulis.

2. Søren Kierkegaard, *Fear and Trembling* and *The Sickness Unto Death* (Garden City, NY: Doubleday Anchor, 1955), p. 88 note.

3. Ibid., pp. 66-67.

4. Jean-Paul Sartre, *Existentialism and Human Emotions* (New York: The Philosophical Library, 1957), p. 19.

5. Kierkegaard, *Fear and Trembling*, p. 35.

6. Ibid., p. 39.

7. Ibid., p. 84.

8. Ibid., p. 90.

9. Ibid., p. 63.

10. Ralph Waldo Emerson, "Heroism," in *Emerson's Essays* (New York: Books, Inc., n.d.), p. 183.

11. *The Wisdom of Ben-Sira* 23a, W. O. E. Oesterley, ed. (London: SPCK, 1916). See John A. Phillips, *Eve: The History of an Idea* (San Francisco: Harper & Row, 1984), p. 38 *ff.*

12. Maurice Friedman, *Problematic Rebel* (revised ed.; Chicago: The University of Chicago Press, 1970).

13. Joseph F. Sagüés, S. J., *De Deo creante et elevante*, No. 393. *Sacrae Theologiae Summa* (Madrid: Biblioteca de autores Cristianos, 1958), Vol. 2, p. 600.

14. Ibid., No. 399.

15. *Eccles.* 10: 15.

16. St. Augustine, *De Civ. Dei*, XII, 6; ML 41, 353.

17. *Genesis* 3:5.

18. Aquinas, *STh* 1, 63, 3. Sagüés, No. 405.

19. Andrew Delbanco, *The Death of Satan* (New York: Farrar, Straus & Giroux, 1995), p. 26.

20. See *The Apocrypha and Pseudoepigrapha of the Old Testament in English*, R. H. Charles, transl. and ed. (Oxford: Clarendon Press, 1913/1969), Vol. 2, pp. 126-127. Also Wilhelm Meyer, ed., "Vita Adae et Evae," *Abhandlungen der Bayerschen Akademie der Wissenschaften: Philosophisch-philologische Classe* 14 (1878): 187-250.

21. St. Augustine, *De Gen. ad lit.*, XI, 14, 18; ML 34, 436.

22. Sagüés, No. 406.

23. Paul Tillich, *Systematic Theology* (Chicago: The University of Chicago Press, 1957), Vol. 2, p. 37 *ff.*

24. *Luke* 10:18.

25. *Luke* 10:20.

26. Joseph A. Fitzmeyer, S. J., *The Gospel According to Luke* (Garden City, NY: Doubleday & Co., Inc., 1985), Vol. 2, p. 860.

27. Matthias Scheeben, *Mysteries of Christianity* (London: Herder & Herder, Co., 1946), p. 261 *ff.*

28. *Inferno* 34: 20, in *Great Books of the Western World*, Robert M. Hutchins, ed. (Chicago: Encyclopaedia Britannica, 1952).

29. Dino S. Cervigni, "Dante's Lucifer: the Denial of the Word," <http://www.brown.edu/departments/italian_studies/ld/numbers/03/cervigni.html>

30. *Paradise Lost*, Book V. 606-608.

31. Book V. 658-662 and VII. 131 *ff.*

32. Book VI. 890 *ff.*

33. G. K. Chesterton, "Lucifer or the Root of Evil" (1929) <http://www.abcog.org/pride.htm>

34. Sūrah 7:11-14. Also Sūrah 2:30-37; 15:27-40; 17: 1-65; 18:50; 20:116; 26:95; 34:20; and 38:71-88. Rūmī, in *Mathnawī* III. 2759 and 3193-98 (London: Luzac, 1925-1940), criticizes Iblīs for having seen only clay in Adam and not the spirit of God in him.

35. Nizamuddīn Awliyā (1236-1325), in his *Fawa'id al-Fu'ad* II, Assembly 25, recounts an anecdote to show how Satan became enthroned in the human heart, beginning with Adam. See Nizam Ad-Din Awliya, *Morals of the Heart*, Bruce B. Lawrence, transl. (New York: Paulist Press, 1992), pp. 164-165. So Rūmī can claim that our human hearts "are houses of Satan" (*Mathnawī* II, 251-252).

36. Rūmī, *Mathnawī*, Book 4, 1, lines 1615-1617.

37. Peter J. Awn, *Satan's Tragedy and Redemption: Iblīs in Sufi Psychology* (Leiden: E. J. Brill, 1983), p. 91.

38. *Qurān* 7:12; 38:76.

39. *Mathnawī*, Book 1, 1, line 3216.

40. Tewfik El Hakim, "The Martyr," in *Arabic Writing Today: The Short Story*, Mahmoud Manzalaoui, ed. (Cairo: American Research Center in Egypt, 1968).

41. Ibid., p. 43.

42. Awn, *Satan's Tragedy and Redemption*, p. 55.

43. 'Ain Al-Qudāt, *Nāmahā* #650, in Awn, *Satan's Tragedy and Redemption*.

44. Ibid., p. 102. This is the case, too, in the story of Abraham and Isaac.

45. As narrated by al-Sarrāj in his *Kitāb al-Luma'*; in Ciryl Glassé, *The Concise Encyclopedia of Islam* (San Francisco: Harper & Row, 1989), p. 166.

46. Quoted in Ibn Al-Jawzī, *Kitāb al-qussās wa 'l-mudhakkirīn*, in Awn, *Satan's Tragedy*, p. 133.

47. Awn, *Satan's Tragedy*, p. 124.

48. El Hakim, "The Martyr," p. 44.

49. Ibid., p. 46.

50. Al-Hallāj, *TāSīn* 9, in *Early Islamic Mysticism*, Michael A. Sells, transl. and ed. (New York: Paulist Press, 1996), p. 274.

51. Sūrah 112 ("al-Iklas").

52. *TāSīn* 11, p. 274.

53. *TāSīn* 12, pp. 274-275.

54. Awn, *Satan's Tragedy*, p. 144, commenting on Ahmed Ghazāli, *Sawānih* #28 and #64.

55. *TāSīn* 14, p. 275.

56. *TāSīn* 15, p. 275-276.

57. *TāSīn* 16, p. 276.

58. Awn, *Satan's Tragedy*, p. 142, explaining 'Ain Al-Qudat's view in his *Tamhīdāt* #287.

59. *TāSīn* 17, p. 276.

60. *Paradise Lost*, Book I.37.

61. Book I.263. Rūmī claims that "Iblīs's sin was innate, so he could not find the way to precious repentance" (*Mathnawī* IV. 3414-15), by which he must mean that the sin occurred so early after creation as to be implicated in his very essence.

62. *Genesis* 22:1-13.

63. Kierkegaard, *Fear and Trembling* and *The Sickness unto Death*, p. 64. Emphasis added.

64. *STh* 1, 64, 3.

65. The closest is the *Felix culpa* ("Lucky sin" or "Happy fault") of the Preface at the end of the "Exultet" sung during the Easter Vigil: "It would have profited us nothing to have been born, unless redemption had also been given to us! O wonderful condescension of your mercy toward us! O inestimable love: to redeem a slave you delivered up your Son! O truly necessary sin of Adam which was blotted out by the death of Christ! O happy fault that merited so great a redeemer!" (*Liber usualis*, ed. by the Benedictines of Solesmes [Tournai, Belgium: Desclée & Co., 1961], p. 776N).

66. *TāSīn* 23, p. 277.

67. See Louis Massignon, *The Passion of al-Hallaj: Mystic and Martyr of Islam* (4 vol.; Princeton, NJ: Princeton University Press, 1982); Gilani Kamran, *Ana al-Haqq Reconsidered* (Lahore: Naqsh-e-Awwal Kitab Ghar, 1398/1987).

68. My own translation from the original Spanish text.

69. Shams ad-Dīn Ahmad Aflākī, *Manāqib al-'Ārifīn* (Virtues of the Knowers) (Tehran: Duniyā-yi Kitāb, 1983), in Sells, *Early Islamic Mysticism*, p. 151.

70. Farīduddīn 'Attār, *Tadhikrat al-'Awliyā'*, Muhammad Istislāmī, ed. (Tehran: Zavvār, 1967), and Nāsir Hayyirī (Tehran: Intishārāt-1 Gulshā'ī, 1982), in Sells, *Early Islamic Mysticism*, p. 169, #53.

4

Faith, Hope, and Unbelief

At the end of his *Tractatus*, Wittgenstein explained what he had tried to accomplish by his book:

> My propositions serve as elucidations in the following way: anyone who understands me eventually recognizes them as nonsensical, when he has used them — as steps — to climb up beyond them. (He must, so to speak, throw away the ladder after he has climbed up it.)
> He must transcend these propositions, and then he will see the world aright.[1]

Centuries before, the Chinese sage Chuang-tzu had said in his typical picturesque style:

> The fish trap exists because of the fish; once you've gotten the fish, you can forget the trap. The rabbit snare exists because of the rabbit; once you've gotten the rabbit, you can forget the snare. Words exist because of meaning; once you've gotten the meaning, you can forget the words. Where can I find a man who has forgotten words so I can have a word with him?[2]

Along similar lines, Buddhist Mahāyāna developed the metaphor of the world (*samsāra*) as a mighty river that must be crossed in a ferryboat (*yāna*). The Buddha is the ferryman, and Buddhist discipline and observance are the ferryboat. But the ferryboat is only a vehicle, an instrument or means for crossing the river, not an eternal necessity that might, even, become an encumbrance. The enlightened person, the one who has thoroughly and profoundly understood, does not continue to carry the raft on his or her back once the crossing is done. On the contrary, says the Buddha.

> Would not the clever man be the one who left the raft (of no use to him any longer) to the current of the stream, and walked ahead without turning back to look at it? Is it not simply a tool to be cast away and forsaken once it has served the purpose for which it was made? . . . In the same way the vehicle of the

doctrine is to be cast away and forsaken, once the other shore of Enlightenment (*nirvāna*) has been attained.[3]

The point, I take it, is that one must move on beyond faith as paradox and enter the realms that have been opened through its help.[4] This is probably also what St. Augustine meant when he said that "it belongs to faith to believe what we do not yet see, and the reward of this faith is to get to see what we have believed."[5]

FAITH AND HOPE

The openness that is faith is maintained and nourished by hope, a human virtue difficult to understand and explain. Hope is the context or medium of faith,[6] what renders faith viable, because without hope, what faith opens itself to would be either prosaic or meaningless, ordinary or irrelevant.

Hope presupposes "being on the way" (*en route*), as does faith; it indicates the expectancy of a journey without definite end or destination; and it points to the human condition as one of travel. To have faith is to be in a journey; to have hope is to be *in statu viatorum* ("in the condition of travelers") for as long as we live, for arrival would be the end of hope as well as the fulfillment of faith.

Hope allows us to maintain an "unresolved openness" toward God, as Moltmann put it.[7] The essence of hope is indeterminate, and this is why it can ground faith. Real hope is not so much the type where we expect a specific outcome, as when we say, for example, "I hope he will come tomorrow," or "I hope we will win." Real hope simply hopes for whatever may arise independently of any possible action on our part.[8] Real hope does not demand, does not foresee, does not involve (in itself) planning, does not hinge on desire, but simply transcends the conditions of life by appealing, in a sense, to "a certain creative power in the world."[9] Hope is possible only beyond the space between knowledge or planning and desire or presumption. To hope is to place one's confidence in a certain power of growth and development to which faith gives access but no guarantee.

In a sense hope is a consciousness of what-is-not-yet, which therefore cannot be fully conceived and must, in consequence, be somehow imagined; not merely of what-is-not-yet, but of what lies beyond, toward which one can only open oneself; that is, not simply what is in the future and therefore not-yet, but what lies beyond our ken and therefore must remain essentially mysterious. In this way hope must be distinguished from a mere orientation to the future, since the beyond is its ultimate justification; and it must be distinguished from action that seeks to change the present for the sake of the future, or to prepare the future in the present, because hope does not merely look at the future which can be somehow glimpsed, imagined, envisioned, but is truly an orientation toward a reality which is beyond all conceiving. Hope does, indeed, desire that reality to come to be, whatever it be, and it may seek to describe it while acknowledging that it cannot be described; hope may even ground a revolutionary activity designed to change the present for the sake of what is yet to be and to make the present a more viable human reality — revolutionary activity is not forbidden by hope; but in the end, even the revolutionary must conclude that what we seek is clouded in the mists of the beyond and that therefore no promise of the future can be concrete and, certainly, cannot be justified by hope alone.

As I said, this does not mean that there is no room for revolutionary activity, for planning, or for the construction of utopian futures. What it does mean is that hoping is an activity different from all these, an activity whose value should not be subordinated to them or its reality judged by their standards.

When Job, in his misery and sickness, exclaims, "I know my vindicator lives . . . and that even with my skin flayed . . . I shall see God,"[10] he is expressing hope in a beyond with God which is not merely future and which is grounded in a resolute faith. Faith, says Moltmann, "believes God to be true, hope awaits the time when this truth shall be manifested."[11] And who can fathom God's time?

One problem with this understanding of hope is that it wrests control from us, and we are often paranoid about being in control. Moreover, we often inadvertently assume that control is always good, when in fact it may not be, for it may elicit insubordination or opposition, which can thwart what we were trying to achieve in the first place.

One of Taoism's basic tenets is the belief in *wu-wei*, "nonaction," the belief that it is possible to obtain the results one wants without actually engaging in direct action: the Sage, says Lao-tzu, "knows without going [anywhere], names without seeing, and completes without doing a thing."[12] This, precisely, is the power of hope.

> Confucius was seeing the sights at Lü-liang, where the water falls from a height of thirty fathoms and races and boils along for forty li, so swift that no fish or other water creature can swim in it. He saw a man dive into the water and, supposing that the man was in some kind of trouble and intended to end his life, he ordered his disciples to line up on the bank and pull the man out. But after the man had gone a couple of hundred paces, he came out of the water and began strolling along the base of the embankment, his hair streaming down, singing a song. Confucius ran after him and said, "At first I though you were a ghost, but now I see you're a man. May I ask if you have some special way of staying afloat in the water?"
>
> "I have no way. I began with what I was used to, grew up with my nature, and let things come to completion with fate. I go under with the swirls and come out with the eddies, following along the way the water goes and never thinking about myself. That's how I can stay afloat."[13]

FAITH AND DOUBT

According to Tillich, "serious doubt is confirmation of faith,"[14] for we do not entertain doubt about what we do not care, and faith is care about what really matters to us. If we are serious about what ultimately concerns us, doubt can never be excluded altogether, but must be faced with courage. Jaspers concurs: "For a thinking believer, one who can understand his faith and find words for it, there is nothing that might not be open to doubt. . . . [F]aith that withstands doubt is real faith."[15]

From this point of view, both the atheist and the unbeliever are not merely people who cannot assent to this or that tenet of a particular religion, or who refuse to belief in God. Rather, unbelief, where it sincerely exists, represents a failure of commitment or an unwillingness to expose oneself to the blustering winds of the future, or of God, or of whatever one is ultimately concerned about. "A faith that does not perpetually expose itself to the possibility of unfaith," wrote Heidegger, "is not faith but merely a convenience: the believer simply makes up his mind to adhere to the traditional doctrine."[16]   Such an adherence to belief or dogma or whatever, rather than reflect intellectual commitment, signifies an indifference to what really matters, to what is of ultimate concern, or an inability to have decidedly ultimate concerns.

That to which faith is an openness is never given wholly to the believer because it is infinite (in time or in essence), absolute, and therefore cannot be grasped by a subject who is finite in every way. This lack of fit between finite and infinite is also the reason why doubt or unfaith is always a danger.   Uncertainty cannot be removed,[17] it must be accepted as the possibility of death is accepted by the soldier who rushes into battle. This is why courage also is a concomitant of faith; not of beliefs in dogmas, which carry security, but of openness to the obscurity of what can be, or of what Is.

Mohammed al-Ghazālī was in his mid-thirties when he was assailed by doubt. There was no question of abandoning his Muslim faith, but of sorting out the valid sources of religious knowledge. As he put it,

> it had already become apparent to me that I had no hope of the bliss of the world to come save through a God-fearing life and the withdrawal of myself from vain desire. It was clear to me too that the key to all this was to sever the attachment of the heart to worldly things by leaving the mansion of deception and returning to that of eternity, and to advance towards God most high with all earnestness.[18]

Gripped by this doubt he gave up his teaching post at Nizāmiyya College in Baghdad and went on a pilgrimage to Mecca, Medina, and Jerusalem, settling down in Damascus for the better part of two years. He finally concluded, with Augustine and Anselm of Canterbury, that one must believe in order to understand,[19] and that only mystical insight can give us the truth of God.

FAITH AND UNBELIEF

There is a sense in which unbelief is salutary. Unbelief can act as a prick to faith, as a gadfly, as Socrates called his questioning. A faith without unbelief may fall asleep, not having to prove itself any longer. In this sense, faith and unbelief are like the yin and yang of self development. According to Jaspers, "without philosophizing, without the situation it creates, I have no chance to make conscious, believing decisions about what I am."[20]

However, not all unbelief is salutary. Stephen Spinks quotes Rümke to the effect that "Belief is something which accompanies us in our development and maturity,"[21] a thesis developed also by Fowler. From this point of view, Rümke maintains, "Unbelief is an interruption of development,"[22] possibly related to the exaggerated narcissism of contemporary individualism. Though this surge of individualism in the modern world is, perhaps, less pronounced in countries where the family and the community still play a large socializing role, it is obviously a near universal factor.

Unbelief is, in a certain sense, also the outcome of secularism; or perhaps not of secularism *per se*, but of its widespread nature. Time was when, at least in Europe and America, the church steeple was the tallest building in the village and the city. Not any more. Our steeples are skyscrapers in which business and military affairs are transacted, not religious ones. Once, even in America, we had our lone "professional" atheists: no more. People who lead their lives as if there were no God are not in the minority today, but seem to be found in all areas of society, and without apology. Years ago the atheist was the odd ball, the stick in the mud: no more. Secularists are the rule rather than the exception, so that a culture of unbelief has been created which now spreads over city, town, and countryside like a morning fog. In this secularism, with its pall of unbelief, no questions of ultimate concern are raised. The only acceptable considerations pertain to the self and the dollar. Or, if one prefers a more optimistic outlook, two forms of ultimate concern clash today in the modern world, the concern for profit and the concern for God, time versus eternity, the finite versus the infinite.[23]

Unbelief need not be atheistic. In fact, it is often most conspicuous among believers, even those who pride themselves on being "good" Christians, Jews, Hindus, or Muslims. Nor is this a matter of hypocrisy. Rather, it is a question of consistency. Millions of believers see no problem in being observant at home but uncaring in the marketplace. Many call themselves "pro-life" but favor war and the death penalty, or profess charity toward all but fail to love the poor and destitute next door. But perhaps most astonishing are the millions of Christians, Jews, Muslims, and Hindus who frequent fundamentalist meetings where their hearts are strangely warmed, and who then walk out into the world with hatred in their hearts and guns in their hands.

In fairness to the atheist I should add that people were often called atheists because they denied *one* concept of the deity, usually the prevalent or the popular one. Socrates was called an atheist because, they said, he did not worship the gods of the city of Athens; the early Christians were called atheists because they refused to worship the Roman gods; for many Muslims, American Christians are the infidel; and Christians have called pagans all those who did not worship the Christian god. From this point of view, we should be thankful to the atheists, because they often force us to confront ideas of the divine we have become accustomed to worship.

MIRACLES AND UNBELIEF

A sign of the prevalence of unbelief is the thirst for miracles, occurrences that defy the laws of nature, or, as St. Augustine said, the laws of nature as we know them.[24] The biblical story of the Hebrews crossing the Red Sea under the leadership of Moses is well known. If ever there was a dramatic story, this is it, and Charlton Heston and the "special effects" people did a magnificent job staging it in the movie, *The Ten Commandments*. But what if the Hebrews did not cross the Red Sea? What if there was a mistranslation of the Hebrew *jam suf*, which means "Reed

Sea"? What if the Hebrews simply forded the marshy, reedy areas north of the Red Sea? And what if they did this at a time when the level of the water at the shore and in the swamps had dropped significantly following the explosion of the island volcano of Thera (now Santorini) in the Aegean Sea? What, in other words, if there was no "miracle" in the usual sense? What if the ancient Hebrews possessed a faith that needed no dramatic intervention by YHWH to bolster it, because they knew how to detect the power of God in ordinary occurrences that just happened when they needed them? What if they were wise enough to believe without miracles?[25]

Why do so many today need "miracles" to believe? It would seem that, contrary to ordinary ways of thinking, "miracles" do not call forth faith as much as they unmask unbelief. For a greater faith is needed to detect the action of the divine in the ebb and flow of ordinary life than would be needed if God, like a Grand Magician, would alter the normal operation of the universe just to dazzle us and convince us of his powers. If there have ever been miracles in the usual sense, perhaps we should be sad that God had to change the order of nature for our sake.

On the other hand, the quest for miracles is the search for certainty, for security. We want guarantees before we commit ourselves. I have often thought that the greatest miracle of antiquity was that Moses, when told to leave Egypt, did not ask God for a road map!

We should learn to spy the hand of God in the most ordinary occurrences of life. A story brings this to the fore:

> One disciple said: "My master stands on one side of the river. I stand on the other holding a piece of paper. He draws a picture in the air and the picture appears on the paper. He works miracles."
> The other disciple said: "My master works greater miracles than that.
> When he sleeps, he sleeps.
> When he eats, he eats.
> When he works, he works.
> When he meditates, he meditates."[26]

Where miracles are not forthcoming, we often take refuge in infallibility. *Roma locuta, causa finita*: once Rome has spoken, the case is closed. How many personal decisions have been forestalled by reference to the authority of the popes!

FAITH AND VIOLENCE

The point here is not the long tradition of associating war with religion and the universality of this association, nor is the point the very notion of "holy war" that was prevalent in ancient Judaism and continues in the Muslim *jihād*, with the Crusades and the Christian wars of reconquest in Spain thrown in for good measure. People of all religions and cultural traditions have had an uncanny way of seeking the justification for their wars in commands from their gods, and this tradition shows no signs of abating. The point I wish to address here concerns the disbelief occasioned by the unparalleled atrocities of the twentieth and twenty-first centuries.

What is peculiar, I think is the facility with which we interrogate God about *our* violence. There is some foundation for this, for, after all, many people believe in an omnipotent God whose providence controls the world. But does the fact that not a sparrow falls dead to earth without the will of God[27] make God responsible for the deaths we deliberately perpetrate?   And if God is omnipotent, where is our freedom?

Again, my point is not the theological discussion of this quandary, a serious problem, indeed, given the Western Judaeo-Christian idea of God, and much ink and blood have been spilled addressing the question. My point is the effect of all the violence on the very belief in God. For example, many people's faith in God was shattered as a result of the Holocaust and the Killing Fields, and this loss of faith is not an inconsiderable factor in the growth of present-day secularism. It is as if we had become disenchanted with a God who cannot still the guns of our enemies or rescue the innocent from the Nazi crematoria and the World Trade Center towers. But then, again, *we* invented this notion of God, and no matter how much sense it may make in philosophy and theology, it is still *our* vision, *our* own understanding of the divinity. If we took God more as the direction toward which we move,[28] or the horizon toward which we open up in faith, allowing the fullness of the unknown and the mystery to dazzle us, we might be more ready to search our own hearts for the malice in them and not lose faith in a God we thankfully cannot fathom or understand. Anselm of Canterbury defined God as that being, than which nothing greater can be conceived,[29] and this awkward sentence gives expression to what we have known all along and St. Augustine verbalized: If we understand, it is not God.[30]

THE VIRTUE OF UNBELIEF

There is something beautiful and inspiring about the certainty of Islamic faith. Sūrah 112 (*al-Ikhlās*) commands a daily test of one's faith: "Say, 'God is One, the Eternal God.' " If one can utter this affirmation every day in one's inmost heart, one is a believer. But by the side of this certainty walks a conviction that if one questions, one may cease to be a believer, therefore one must not question. If one questions, one is not a believer, one is not totally submissive to God. Salman Rushdie questioned and he was excommunicated, and a price was put on his head.

It is not only in Islam that certainty is pushed to an extreme. In Amsterdam, the Portuguese Jew Benedict de Espinoza questioned and was excommunicated, a *herem* pronounced against him by his own Jewish community. Such was the fate, too, of Luther, and more recently, of Father Curran and of Hans Küng.

It is well to remember that "heresy" (αἵρεσις) in classical Greek means choice, plan, purpose, but in New Testament Greek it begins to be used to designate a faction, a school of thought, and is applied to the new followers of Jesus ("the sect of the Nazarenes"[31]), who in turn used it for the dissenters and factions in their midst.[32]

In all this certainty unbelief — or perhaps, simply, doubt — plays an important role, for where there is absolute certainty and unexaminedness, the suspicion must lurk that something is being hidden, some fissure is being plastered over, some weakness is being covered up by a conspiracy of silence.[33] Unbelief helps people begin the process of examination of their own beliefs on the assumption, sensible from any point of view, that there are mistaken beliefs. But rather than counsel the examination of all beliefs, or the doubting of all beliefs (as al-Ghazālī and Descartes proposed), the suggestion is made that each believer seek, honestly and earnestly, to discover at least one mistaken belief. Such a discovery would lead to the questioning of other beliefs, or at least to the realization that one is not infallible. One might also come to see that holding a false belief is not the fault of the belief but of the believer: *we* are at fault, *we* are the duped, the biased, the credulous, the fanatics, who need to look into our own hearts to extirpate from them the weeds of untruth.[34] From this point of view unbelief may be turned into that virtue which, Socrates said, makes life worth living.[35] Unbelief, thus, may pave the way out of fanaticism, or, if practiced assiduously, it may even prevent it. Perhaps we need to institute in all centers of religious studies an academic cathedra of unbelief!

FAITH AND PRAYER

It should be cause for thinking that most non-Western traditions do not speak so much of prayer as of meditation and contemplation. Not that prayer of petition is entirely absent, but that it does not have the importance it seems to have in our Western, especially Christian, cultures. And it is well that this should be the case, for prayer of petition, or even prayer of intercession and thanksgiving, is far removed from the openness to the Divine that contemplation encourages. At the beginning of his book on prayer, Hans Urs von Balthasar says,

> Prayer is something more than an exterior act performed out of a sense of duty, an act in which we tell God various things he already knows, a kind of daily attendance in the presence of the Sovereign who awaits, morning and evening, the submission of his subjects.[36]

The truth is that if we paused to think about the assumptions that support prayer of petition, we would be horrified. For instance, to petition God and expect that he will grant our prayers is to assume that God can be suaded — which means that prayers have power over him, denying his omnipotence; or that he does not know what is going on, which denies his omniscience; or that he does not care about us and about the world "but sits above his handiwork, invisible, refined out of existence, indifferent, paring his fingernails,"[37] which would deny his infinite mercy. Prayer of petition, therefore, uncovers our very warped notion of God, and it acts more as a cover up for our ignorance and laziness than as a real approach to God and his caring will. It even exposes a paranoia about control, as if we could not stand uncertainty but had to shield ourselves from it at all costs. Moreover, it is as if we were desperate for control of the unknown in our lives, so we act as we do when we shake a pin ball machine hoping against hope to control the outcome of the game. In a sense, prayer of petition arises from the same urge to cheat our way to the desired outcome, not the one Providence will dispense to us unawares. As Moschner says, "we would not need to philosophize at length about the asking of things from God were not its manner and attitude so often fundamentally wrong."[38]

It might be said that prayers of petition do more to delude the petitioner than to establish contact with God, for in truth, as Dionysus explained, the petitioner is deceived in the same way as a sailor pulling on a rope made fast to a rock. To the sailor in the boat the rock looks as if it is coming towards him in answer to his effort, when in fact, the rock, like the will of God, is immovable.[39]

But take faith as essentially a paradoxical turning toward what ultimately concerns us, as the direction toward that which lies beyond us, and prayer acquires a new meaning. It is simply *looking in that direction*. Prayer is, says Balthasar, "an inward gaze into the depths of the soul and, for that very reason, beyond the soul to God,"[40] who is the soul's ultimate concern.

> It is an unwavering "gaze," where "looking" is always "hearing"; for what is looked at is the free and infinite Person who, from the depths of his freedom, is able to give himself in a manner ever new, unexpected and unpredictable.[41]

CONCLUSION

Sincere believers, then, whose lives are hooked to God become, in turn, a projection of God's image. Jesus said once to Philip, "Anyone who has seen me has seen the Father,"[42] and in a *Hadīth* Mohammed said, "He who has seen me has seen the Truth" (*al-Haqq*); hence it follows that to know Jesus or the Prophet is to know God.

True believers, as Gregory of Nazianzus (*ca.*330-389) said — though he feared his words might offend — are "divinized," so that God deals with them "more familiarly, as with His relatives . . . united and known to them as God to gods."[43] When Christians were martyred in Lyons around 177, they saw in their sister Baldina, hung on a post, the One who was crucified for them.[44]

In Islam, Bāyazīd (Abū Yazīd Tayfūr) al-Bistāmī (died 874), maintained that in ecstasy the empirical self is totally annihilated in God.[45] Al-Sarrāj quoted him as saying, "Lovers do not attain to the reality of love until the one says to the other, 'O thou I.' "[46] Again, al-Sarrāj preserved a prayer of Abū Yazīd:

> Adorn me with thy unity and clothe me with thy I-ness and raise me up unto thy oneness, so that when the creatures see me, they may say, "We have seen thee and thou art that." Yet I [Abū Yazīd] will not be there at all.[47]

So Jesus praised those who were able to see Him in his needy followers,[48] and 'Attār (died 1229) described for us the unforgettable scene in which the birds, after their trials and tribulations, were finally addressed by the divine Simurgh, who told them without speaking:

> The sun of my majesty is a mirror. He who sees himself therein sees his soul and his body, and sees them completely. . . . Although you are now completely changed you see yourselves as you were before. . . . All that you have known, all that you have seen, all that you have said or heard — all this . . . you did by my action. . . . All that you have heard or seen or known is not even the beginning of what you must know, and since the ruined habitation of this world is not your

place you must renounce it. Seek the trunk of the tree, and do not worry about whether the branches do or do not exist.[49]

NOTES

1. Ludwig Wittgenstein, *Tractatus Logico-Philosophicus* (London: Routledge & Kegan Paul, 1961), 6. 54, p. 151.

2. Chuang-tzu, *The Complete Works of Chuang-tzu*, Burton Watson, transl. (New York: Columbia University Press, 1968), p. 302.

3. *Majjhima-Nikāya* 3. 2. 22. 135, in Heinrich Zimmer, *Philosophies of India* (New York: Meridian, 1951), p. 478.

4. In *I Corinthians* 13:13, St. Paul claims that faith, hope, and love last for ever, which would make no sense for faith and hope once heaven is gained; for according to belief, in heaven one would need no faith (since God, the object of faith, would be present) and no hope (since there would be nothing more to expect). The function and nature of faith, then, must be altered if it is to remain for ever. This is the point I am trying to make here.

5. St. Augustine, *Sermo* 43, 1; ML 38, 254.

6. Jürgen Moltmann, *Theology of Hope* (New York: Harper & Row, 1967), p. 16. The contemporary literature on hope is challenging. Besides Moltmann's work, there is Ernst Bloch's monumental *The Principle of Hope* (3 vols.; Cambridge, MA: MIT Press, 1986); Josef Pieper, *On Hope*, Mary M. McCarthy, transl. (San Francisco: Ignatius Press, 1986); and Gabriel Marcel, *Homo Viator* (New York: Harper Torchbooks, 1962).

7. Moltmann, *Theology of Hope*, p. 22.

8. Marcel, *Homo Viator*, p. 41.

9. Ibid., p. 52.

10. *Job* 19:25-26.

11. Moltmann, *Theology of Hope*, p. 20.

12. Lao-tzu, *Tao Te Ching* 47; Robert G. Henricks, transl. and ed., *Lao-tzu Te-Tao Ching* (New York: Ballantine Books, 1989), p. 16.

13. *Chuang-tzu* 19, in *The Complete Works of Chuang-tzu*, pp. 204-205.

14. Paul Tillich, *Dynamics of Faith* (New York: Harper Torchbooks, 1958), p. 22.

15. Karl Jaspers, *Philosophy* (3 vols.; Chicago: The University of Chicago Press, 1969), Vol. 1, p. 255.

16. Martin Heidegger, *An Introduction to Metaphysics* (New York: Doubleday Anchor Books, 1961), p. 6.

17. Tillich, *Dynamics of Faith*, p. 16.

18. Mohammed al-Ghazālī, *Al-Munqidh min al-dalāl* (Deliverance from Error), transl. by Montgomery Watt as *The Faith and Practice of Al-Ghazali* (London: George Allen & Unwin, Ltd., 1953), III. 126, p. 56.

19. St. Augustine, *De libero arbitrio* II, 2, 6; ML 32, 1243; Anselm of Canterbury, *Proslogium; Monologium; An Appendix on Behalf of the Fool by Gaunilon; and Cur Deus Homo*, Sidney Norton Dean, transl. (Chicago: The Open Court Publishing Co., 1939), Ch. 1, p. 7.

20. Jaspers, *Philosophy*, Vol. 1, p. 256.

21. H. C. Rümke, *The Psychology of Unbelief* (London: Rockliff, 1952), p. xi, quoted in G. Stephens Spinks, *Psychology and Religion* (Boston: Beacon Press, 1967), p. 184.

22. Ibid.

23. Tillich, *Dynamics of Faith*, p. 124.

24. St. Augustine, *De civ. Dei* XXI, 8, 2-5; ML 41, 721-722.

25. "Who would deny that none of this is necessary to the wise?" St. Augustine, *De utilitate credendi* 16, 34; ML 42, 89.

26. From *The Fire of Silence and Stillness*, Paul Harris, ed. (Springfield, IL: Templegate Publishers, 1997), p. 103, quoted in *Parabola* 22:4 (November, 1997), p. 49. Also in Paul Reps, ed., *Zen Flesh, Zen Bones* (Garden City, NY: Doubleday Anchor, n. d.), No. 80, p. 68.

27. *Matthew* 10:29.

28. Huston Smith, *Why Religion Matters* (San Francisco: HarperCollins, 2001), p. 3.

29. Anselm of Canterbury, *Proslogium*, Ch. 2, p. 7.

30. St. Augustine, *Sermo* 117, 3, 5; ML 38, 663.

31. *Acts* 24:5.

32. See, for example, *1 Corinthians* 11:19.

33. Kenneth Cragg, *The House of Islam* (2nd ed.; Belmont, CA: Wadsworth Publishing Co., 1975), p. 124.

34. Bernard J. F. Lonergan, *Insight: A Study of Human Understanding* (New York: Philosophical Library, 1967), pp. 716-717.

35. Plato, *Apology* 38A.

36. Hans Urs von Balthasar, *Prayer* (New York: Paulist Press, 1967), p. 11.

37. James Joyce, *A Portrait of the Artist as a Young Man* (New York: The Viking Press, 1958), p. 215.

38. Franz M. Moschner, *Christian Prayer* (New York: B. Herder Book Co., 1962), p. 37.

39. H. Van Zeller, *The Inner Search* (Garden City, NY: Image Books, 1967), p. 71.

40. Von Balthasar, *Prayer*, p. 20.

41. Ibid.

42. *John* 14:9.

43. θεὸς θεοῖς ἐνούμενός (*Orat.*38,7).

44. Eusebius, *Historia Ecclsesiastica* (The History of the Church) (New York: Barnes & Noble, 1995), V, 1, 41.

45. Abū Nasr Al-Sarrāj, *Kitāb al-Luma' fī l-Tasawwuf*, R. A. Nicholson, ed. (Leyden: E.J. Brill, 1914), in R.C. Zaehner, *Hindu and Muslim Mysticism* (New York: Schocken Books, 1969), p. 93.

46. al-Sarrāj 384, quoted in Zaehner, pp. 13-14.

47. al-Sarrāj 382, in Zaehner, p. 94.

48. *Matthew* 25:34-46.

49. Farīduddīn 'Attār, *Mantiq al-Tayr* (The Conference of the Birds) (Boston: Shambhala, 1993), 45.

5

Faith, Dogma, and Fanaticism

The equation of faith with the "what" of belief, with belief statements and prescriptions — "belief *that*" rather than, simply, "belief" or "belief *in*" — is not without consequence because it tends to lead to rigid adherence to the particular statements. In this way dogmatism is born, an extreme but common form of which is fanaticism. It should be noted that fanaticism is not only a religious aberration. Holding with absolute narrowness and tenacity to extreme beliefs is common in the realm of politics as much as in religion. Similarly, fanaticism is not only a matter of adherence to belief. As William James has shown, it appears also when there is an exaggerated allegiance to a person. This prompted James to define fanaticism as "loyalty carried to a convulsive extreme."[1] Moreover, "True believers," as Hoffer called them, are to be found in all walks of life. The task of the present chapter is to analyze in some detail the characteristics of fanaticism as one of the dangers accruing to the rigid adherence to dogma.

FANATICISM AND FAITH

Hoffer begins his book, *The True Believer*,[2] with a quotation from Pascal's *Pensées*[3] who finds the root of fanaticism in our own embarrassment at not being all we would like to be. With a kind of *réssentiment*[4] we turn against the truth that exposes our untruth, and would rather veil it from us than have it mirror our shortcomings. Blind faith has no eyes to see the complex truth, for that would be its demise; so all fanatics are willing to die basically for the same thing, blotting the truth. "True believers" are unwilling ever to confront their own obscurity, religious or otherwise, for it is themselves they seek under cover of religion, social welfare, nationalism, or revolution.

Fanaticism is not merely a matter of theoretical belief. Fanatics pursue their ideas in utter disregard of the interests of others. Hoffer suggests that fanatics find in their absolute assurance about dogma or cause a substitute for their own insecurities. This is a major reason why they cling so passionately to whatever they embrace, and why they can move effortlessly from one extreme cause to another:

the nature of the cause is not as significant as the disguise of their insecurity.[5] For this reason, too, most fanatics are future oriented; they love utopian projects. Being concerned with the future they need not contend with the present and its uncertainties and ambiguities.

In a very real sense fanaticism is a form of absolute freedom. Writing against the background of the French Revolution, Hegel claimed that when an individual abstracts him or herself from everything in a society and identifies wholly only with the universal, the world, including people, becomes subsumed under this consciousness but with no voice of its own or rights different from the individual's. In these conditions the individual, plenipotentiary of his or her absolute realm but unable to join others or to participate in their endeavors because they have been blotted out of the meaningful world, will terrorize without remorse:

> In this absolute freedom all social ranks or classes . . . are effaced and annulled; the individual consciousness that belonged to any such group and exercised its will and found its fulfillment there, has removed the barriers confining it; its purpose is the universal purpose, its language universal law, its work universal achievement.[6]

At this point no conciliation or compromise is possible, and wrath and destruction ensue. Concerned about our own future because of the reigning individualism of our culture, J. Glenn Gray writes: "If this mood [of exaggerated individualism] continues to deepen in our populace it could result in a mad fury of destruction with meaningless death as an essential consequence of such strife."[7] Current events have proved these words prophetic.

Writing about fanaticism in a more analytical sense, Richard Hare makes a distinction between ideals and interests. One basic difference between the two is that ideals are universalizable while interests are not because they are wholly dependent on nurture and idiosyncracy, which are unique to each of us. Ideals depend on reasons which, quâ reasons, are universalizable, but the ultimate justification of an interest is that "I like it," and this is not sufficient to make a universal generalization. For example, I can wish everyone to be happy because the ideal of universal happiness is reasonable, but I cannot expect everyone to like onions. Universal happiness is an ideal; liking onions is an acquired interest, and therefore it is not universalizable.

Ideals and interests are most often treated differently, and a close inspection of them easily reveals their separate spheres. In certain cases, however, ideals and interests combine in such a way as to create a problem. Thus, for example, I may have a lofty ideal and *an interest in having it fulfilled*, but this interest may conflict with the interests of others in fulfilling their own ideals. It is here that potentially serious conflicts arise: my interest in pursuing my ideal may interfere with other people's interests in pursuing theirs; and since interests are not universalizable, the essential condition for being tolerant is absent, and where tolerance and rational argument are excluded, violence is almost always inevitable.[8]

The usual solution to this quandary is to commit oneself to one's ideals and their pursuit only as long as this pursuit does not interfere with other people's pursuit of their ideals. This entails giving everyone's ideals the same weight *as ideals.*[9] A balance is thus achieved in practice, but when this balance is transgressed, fanaticism occurs.

This balance, which we often refer to as tolerance, is relatively easy to commit to in theory. Yet, at the same time, it is also easy to find in history examples of fanaticism which appear to have been enlightened and successful. The intolerance of our Founding Fathers toward the abuses of King George, the intolerance of Gandhi for the conditions imposed by the British in India, the intolerance of Martin Luther King, Jr., for the denial of civil rights to blacks in America, all were successful and, in retrospect, morally justified instances of absolute adherence to a creed at the expense of the interests of others, so the question arises whether some forms of fanaticism are ever justifiable, or, on the contrary, whether all types of fanaticism must be judged morally wrong — and, conversely, whether tolerance is always an unmixed blessing.

In a brilliant essay Marcuse[10] argued that the ideals of tolerance break down in the concrete lives of governments and societies. Tolerance today, he wrote, is commonly shown by people toward government and its practices, many of which are inhumane and unethical. Government, in turn, tolerates opposition to itself only within the established, traditional frameworks. Thus righteous citizens are made to tolerate evil so that the structure itself may be preserved; but by dissenting within the system they tend to become the system to the degree that they work within it.

In other words, ideally, tolerance must be an end in itself, not subservient to any established order or disestablished opposition; otherwise it is always limited *de facto*. But, argues Marcuse, societies need to recreate constantly the conditions for a more humanized life. The problem is *not* one of realizing individual freedom within an existing structure, but of creating a structure that will not stifle individual freedom. In this task, the "pure tolerance" outlined above is of no use, for it tolerates error and evil as well as truth and goodness. In some ways, then, tolerance must become intolerant toward evil and error, for "the telos of tolerance is truth."[11] But how does one know *the* truth? Ideally, as a precondition, by having access to *all* sources of information; but this is *de facto* negated by our existing democratic structures. This is the reason why "pure tolerance" — the tolerance described above — is itself a failure as an ideal. Not that one must therefore prefer fanaticism, but that "pure tolerance" is not an automatic antidote to fanaticism. And to complicate matters, there is the historical fact that some fanatical acts are considered holy in certain traditions. I shall consider a few examples here.

On the face of it, the women who burn themselves to death on the funeral pyres of their husbands in India (*satīs*), martyrs in various religious traditions, kamikaze pilots, Palestinian suicide bombers, and Buddhist monks setting themselves on fire, are all fanatics: they commit to their ideals in an absolute, uncompromising way. They are like the dogmatists of all religious and political persuasions. The difference is that while most fanatics commit themselves in theory to the principle that in the pursuit of their ideals they ought to sacrifice the interests of others even if this included the sacrifice of their own interests, terrorists, martyrs, and *satīs* actually concretize this commitment by committing suicide in pursuit of their ideals. Is their fanaticism morally justified?

SATĪS : DEATH BY FIRE

Hinduism distinguishes several types of suicide, only one of which, so-called desperation suicide, is absolutely condemned. Other suicides are deemed legitimate. Among these must be included the mass suicides of officials upon the death of their master or king, and the self-immolation of heroes in battle when the odds were clearly against them. These suicides, whether devotional or connected with one's official tasks, are conceived in terms of the commitment the men have vowed, either to their masters or to their commanders as soldiers.

The most notorious example of suicide in India is *satī*, the self-immolation of a widow on the funeral pyre of her dead husband. *Satī* has been practiced in India since time immemorial. Muslim rulers allowed the practice to continue because they considered it a religious ritual in which they should not interfere, and the British did the same, at least initially, and for the same reasons. But the atrocity of the spectacle became too much for the Europeans, and their own complicity weighed heavily on them. In the face of some 654 *satīs* in 1821, and of 583 in 1822, and after intensive lobbying by Rām Mohan Roy and others, the practice was outlawed in 1829. It did not disappear completely, but the numbers were greatly reduced. Between 1943 and 1987, for example, there were thirty *satīs* in Rajasthan alone and some forty nation-wide since Independence. Since 1988 all glorification of *satīs* has been forbidden.[12]

Self-immolation in the funeral pyres of their husbands is something only women are expected to do, just as heroism in battle even unto death is something only men are expected to do, "since within the context of marriage, tradition only acknowledges the love of wives for their husbands — love being a woman's duty."[13] One could almost say that war is to men as love is to women.

The term *satī* denotes the woman, not the act of self-immolation. There is no special term for the act. The root of the word is Sanskrit *as-* ("to be"), from which comes *sat* ("what is" [*m.*]), and *satī* ("what is" [*f.*]). In the act, the divine goddess (*Shakti*) irrupts, becomes present ("is") in this world in the person of the *satī* , invoked by the repetition of the mantra *sat*. As the *satī* plunges into the fire, her physical personality is extinguished instantly and without suffering by the inner presence of the divine. This passage is shielded from view by the fire raging around her. Ideally, this fire should have been lighted from the domestic fire burning in the hearth, originally kindled at the time of her wedding.[14]

There are two ways of becoming a *satī* : (1) joint cremation (*sahagamana* or s*ahamarana*) and (2) deferred cremation (*anugamana* or *anumarana*), for in some cases, and for a variety of circumstances, the self-immolation is postponed. A woman who undergoes "the madness of the *sat,*"[15] but does not die because, for example, she is prevented, or is extricated from the flames by official police action (since the act is illegal), becomes a "living *satī* ," that is, a holy woman. Conversely, a *satī* cannot go through with her act if she has been polluted by contact with a *shudra*, with the color indigo, with a foreigner, or by menstruation. In fact, the list of impediments is rather large.[16] Moreover, attempts may be made to dissuade her, more so now than in ancient times, where they appeared to be *pro forma*. In some cases where efforts to prevent the *satī* from going through with her resolve created a true obstacle, "trial by fire" was employed, usually at the insistence of the woman herself. The model is that of Sītā, who underwent the ordeal in order to prove that she had been loyal to her husband Rāmā during her abduction and imprisonment.[17]

A woman must *declare* her resolve (*samkalpa*) to become a *satī*, and once declared, she may not recant.[18] The resolve may have been adumbrated years before the actual occasion: as a girl or young woman, she may have foreseen a future in which she would immolate herself in her husband's pyre, or may have expressed a rare attraction for fire. The "feeling" or "emotion" (*bhāv*) of the *sat* that eventually will precipitate her into the flames may have been incipient in her: "Like a fire brooding beneath the embers, it remains in a latent state until the day it discloses itself in the *bhāv*."[19]

How to understand these fanatical women who become *satīs*? Some have seen in them an interesting example of what Durkheim called "altruistic suicide." Altruistic suicide takes place when society is too binding, when there is an exaggerated collectivism, and, consequently, too rudimentary a sense of individuality. In such circumstances the result is fanaticism, the blind surrender to something outside the self, "where the ego is not its own property, where it is blended with something not itself, where the goal of conduct is exterior to itself."[20]

> We actually see the individual in all these cases seek to strip himself of his personal being in order to be engulfed in something which he regards as his true essence. . . . He feels that he exists in it and in it alone, and strives so violently to blend himself with it in order to have being. He must therefore consider that he has no life of his own. Impersonality is here carried to its highest pitch; altruism is acute. . . . [Suicide, in this case] springs from hope; for it depends on the belief in beautiful perspectives beyond this life. It even implies enthusiasm and the spur of a faith eagerly seeking satisfaction, affirming itself by acts of extreme energy.[21]

While this understanding offers a perspective, it leaves out the inner motivation of the *satī*.

In Hinduism, caste provides the basic context for all self-perception. Since caste is established by birth, by birth one belongs to a specific group, guild or craft, and therefore one is no longer free to choose how to respond to events in one's life. But within the objective setting of the caste there is a subjective moral obligation to find out the duties of one's state in life as husband, wife, merchant, and so on; that is, there is an obligation to embark on a voyage of self-discovery within the bounds set by birth — "to become who one is," as Nietzsche would put it. The confluence of the objective setting of caste with the subjective moral obligation is what is meant by *dharma*, "duty." By doing this, one allows "being" (*sat*) to appear or be fulfilled as "truth" (*satya*) in one's life, a truth which obviously transcends individuality. Thus one becomes *sat* (male) or *satī* (female). The role of every husband and wife (within their caste) is to exemplify or reenact the transcendental relationship between Shiva and Shakti, the divine pair; the divine reality (*sat*) is constituted by both Shiva and Shakti in their eternal embrace: therefore it should not be possible to conceive of Shiva without Shakti any more than it should be to conceive of a wife without her husband. When the husband dies, the wife becomes "unreal" (*a–sat*). In this ontological imbalance, the moral duty (*dharma*) for the wife to immolate herself with her husband may have arisen. As the *Gītā* (3:35) put it, "Better your own *dharma* imperfectly performed than another's *dharma* perfectly performed." In this context it is to be noted that the majority of *satīs* have been from the kshatriya caste and among Rājputs, for whom the sense of duty is extremely powerful.

But there are other motivational factors of equal or even greater importance. For example, one should not discount the often-overwhelming power of example. Satī, the name given now to the self-sacrificial wife, is the name of Shiva's first wife. She burned herself with the fire of her own yoga (*yogāgni*) to avenge the fact that her husband, Shiva, had not been invited by her own father to a special ritual ceremony.[22] The *satī*, therefore, is an incarnation or *avatār* of the goddess, of the *Shakti*. She is a manifestation of the divine female power. Her sacrificial act is involved in the mystery of all manifestations of the divine, and remains, as such, essentially unfathomable. As Raghubir Singh Rathor put it, "To be sure, it is human nature to wish to put a stop to the sacrifices of satīs. Yet sometimes we find ourselves faced with *śaktis* who, when they reveal their extraordinary nature, make us forget the fine dictates of reason."[23]

Still, the *satī* is obviously a fanatic, but given her profound religious motivation, can one be certain that this fanaticism is morally wrong? And is it different from the fanaticism of the suicidal terrorist?[24]

THE CHRISTIAN MARTYRS

Despite its repudiation of voluntary suicide, Christianity offers us in its martyrs a case parallel to that of the *satīs*; most Christian martyrs were willing victims, but some of them surrendered to their deaths with an exuberance that almost bordered on suicide. First we to look for an ideology that becomes exaggerated in the martyr's readiness to die what often was a horrible death.

Christian behavior and Christian conscience cannot be separated from the *koinonia*, the Christian community. The guidance derived from the connatural awareness of what God is doing can never be complete until God's purposes are discovered within the *koinonia*; and this for the simple reason that the *koinonia* is but an extension of Christ; in fact, the Christ's "body." The full discovery of, love for, and identification with the total Christ, must necessarily include the Christ's "body," the *koinonia*. For this, the conscience must be *theonomous* ("God-normed"), in Lehmann's words.[25] Given the *theonomous* character of conscience, the moral action flowing from it is the fruit of a "connatural" awareness of what God is doing. In other words, for the Christian, moral behavior flows from a loving identification with the living Christ, from an *imitatio Christi* which is the result of a quasimystical, connatural knowledge and love of Christ.

Having this "knowledge" or awareness of God's purposes,[26] Christians simply "act out" what they *are*, namely, Christians, spiritual people. When such an identification is achieved, martyrdom is endured as the only way of acting Christianly in the circumstances. Thus, for example, Felicitas, martyred in 203, had been pregnant at the time of her incarceration and trial, and she gave birth while in jail a few days before her death. As her chronicler narrates,

> she suffered a good deal in her labor because of the natural difficulty of an eight
> months' delivery. And hence one of the prison guards said to her:
> "You are suffering so much now — what will you do when you are tossed to
> the beasts?"
> And she replied, "What I am suffering now I suffer by myself. But then
> another will be inside of me, who will suffer for me, because I am to suffer for
> Him."[27]

When Perpetua's turn came to be killed, the soldier's hand struck the bone, and
she screamed. Then she recovered and "took the wavering hand of the young
gladiator and guided it to her throat . . . [as if she] could not be killed unless she
herself was willing."[28]

Eusebius has kept another account, this time of the martyrs of Lyons, executed
in 177-178. Quoting from an extant narrative, he writes:

> Blandina was hung on a post as food for the wild beasts let loose on the arena.
> She looked as if she was hanging from a cross, and through her ardent prayers she
> stimulated great enthusiasm in those undergoing their ordeal, who in their agony
> saw with their outward eyes in the person of their sister the One who was crucified
> for them, that He might convince those who believe in Him that any man who has
> suffered for the glory of Christ has fellowship for ever with the living God.[29]

The martyrs were raised to a state beyond their natural powers, one in which, as
they believed, they were sustained by the grace of God, and thus strengthened to
suffer any kind of pain. In this respect, and in their theological explanation, they
are not very different from the *satīs*.

In both instances we see the individuals (to paraphrase Durkheim) stripped of
their personal being in order to be engulfed in something which they regard as their
true essence. When this is the case, both traditions consider suicide morally
justified, though for different reasons. Hinduism places the *satī* squarely in the
realm of the transcendent, since in the *satī* the *Shakti* becomes both visible and
operative. Christianity regards the martyr as only indirectly a suicide, and it places
the inspiration also squarely in the realm of the divine imitation.

But in point of fact martyrs, like *satīs*, are fanatics, for they cling to their ideals
absolutely and at the expense of the interests of others, parents, lovers, and society
at large. And is this type of fanaticism any more tolerable and justifiable than that
of the terrorists?

THE TERRORIST

There *is* a significant difference between the terrorist and other fanatics: the
terrorist instills terror and commits murder, the deliberate killing of innocent
people, often for seemingly flimsy reasons. Yet the case is not clear cut, for the
intention of the terrorist, as that of the fanatic, must be taken into account.

Since ancient times, the case of Samson has been a paradigm, for it is claimed
that Samson did not kill himself to kill others (his suicide was not voluntary), but,

rather, killed others to avenge his humiliation and blindness at the hands of the Philistines — and in the process lost his life. Milton, in *Samson Agonistes*, claims that Samson died, "Not willingly, but tangl'd in the fold/Of dire necessity,"[30] a view compatible with *Judges* 16:28.

Samson's case makes clear the difficulty of interpretation: his story is told by his family and friends, but we do not know how the Philistines felt about his terrorist act. In our times, we often have both sides of the terrorist's story but no clear guidelines to interpret it — except, perhaps, its consequences. Even then, as Maritain showed, the moral nature of a physical act changes when the situation to which it belongs becomes so different that it can no longer be judged by the usual standards. Such is the case in repressive societies, concentration camps, states of siege, and ghettos.[31] Does the case of the modern terrorist fall within these parameters?

One must add that a major problem in understanding terrorism and violence is that violence is universal. It exists among the lawful and the unlawful, the high and the low, the rich and the poor, among those who seek to justify it (and themselves) and among those who do not.[32]

FANATICISM AND REVOLT

Among the memorable literary images of fanaticism must stand The Renegade, a man without a name, whose long soliloquy is the text of Camus's short story, "The Renegade."[33] The Renegade is a man who trained to be a Catholic missionary. In school he came to believe with fanatical force that Catholicism was the sun that illumined the whole world. It took time to accept this as *the* truth: his teachers said he was bright but pig-headed — "Bull-headed," his father used to say. In seminary he conceived the idea of becoming the best missionary he could be. This was the only idea that really gripped him, and since he was stubborn, he decided to carry it to its logical conclusion: he determined to go to the worst, most isolated, most savage, most inauspicious and barbarous village to evangelize the cruel, faithless people who dwelled there.

And so he did. He was received unceremoniously, beaten, tortured, and locked up in the House of the Fetish, the god that ruled over the villagers. After weeks of starving he was ritually consecrated to the Fetish, his tongue was cut out, and he was left to ponder what had become of his life. In the end, he began to pray to the Fetish, convinced that It was the only god, and as the weeks passed, his devotion to the Fetish grew until it became as absolute as his commitment to Christ had been. As a pig-headed fanatic, he had simply changed gods, and he held to the new one with the same tenacity he had held to the old.

The end came when, in a fanatical rage, he shot down the missionary who was coming to the village to take his place. He was beaten again and left in the desert to die, wondering, in the jumble of his dreams, if perhaps he had been wrong again.

This kind of fanaticism is developed again in Camus's play, "The Just Assassins."[34] The play concerns the historical attempts of a group of revolutionaries in Russia to assassinate the Grand Duke Sergei in 1905. A major figure in the play is Stepan, a man who had once been apprehended by the police, tortured, and confined to jail, from which he had eventually escaped to Switzerland. Now he has returned to carry on his original revolutionary activity. But torture has turned Stepan into a fanatic. For him, there is no love. There are no limits, either. There is nothing forbidden if it may foster the revolution. He believes in the values he and his companions stand for even if it means forcing them down on complacent humanity. To those who disagree, he answers, "You don't believe in the revolution, any of you."[35]

The taunt is addressed to all, though the focus is Ivan Kaliayev, a young poet who has joined the revolution because he loves life. He is charged with throwing the bomb when the Grand Duke attends the theater, but noticing the children in the company of their father, Kaliayev refrains and returns to the revolutionary hideout: killing innocent children is a limit he will not cross. Discussions ensue, passionate and philosophical, for the question is whether or not murder is *ever* morally justified.

This is not an easy matter to settle. To kill another human being violates the ethics of respect for human life that should be — and is, at least theoretically — at the base of all revolutions. But to stand by while others debase, murder, and execute people is not just shameful, it makes one a collaborator, an accomplice. Kaliayev's solution — kill only when absolutely necessary and then accept your own death as proof that murder is not permitted — may not appear reasonable or satisfactory to many. But in fact, that is exactly what happened historically: in his next try, Kaliayev did hurl the bomb that killed the Grand Duke, and then he stood by, without attempting to flee, while the police grabbed him and led him to jail. He was eventually hanged and his death, his comrades felt, lifted the pall of murder from their act: they felt justified.

It should be clear, of course, that Kaliayev's reason for joining the revolution is often the moral justification offered by suicide terrorists. And there is no reason to doubt it. It presents itself also as an alternative to fanaticism. Che Guevara, in 1965, gave expression to the same feeling: "Let me say, with the risk of appearing ridiculous, that the true revolutionary is guided by strong feelings of love. It is impossible to think of an authentic revolutionary without this quality."[36] This is, perhaps, a better justification of violence and terrorism than that offered in the name of the future: the justification of violence and terrorism by reference to the future is invalid simply because of the contingency of the future.[37]

But the problem of means remains, and since revolt is necessary in order to ensure the humanizing of all societies, the problem is not likely to go away any time soon — unless we take pains to prevent fanaticism and extend the reign of love. Al-Ghazālī has preserved for us a comment of the Prophet: on returning to Medina after a battle, he remarked, "We have returned from the lesser jihad to the greater jihad." When asked what he meant, he replied, "Struggling against the enemy in your own breast."[38]

WHY FANATICISM ?

Given the nature of fanaticism and the consequences it leads to, it is legitimate to ask why it should continue to reappear in the world, whether in the realm of politics or in that of religion, whether as adherence to leading dogmas or to dogmatic leaders. The question is significant, but it may be impossible to give an answer that encompasses all types of fanaticism or that is universally satisfying. Moreover, as has been pointed out, it is often difficult to distinguish between genuine commitment to an ideal and fanatical pursuit of the same. In the view of many, the *satī* is a fanatic, and so is the martyr. Again, for many, suicide terrorists are fanatics, while for others their motivation is genuine, and they are considered heroes. Moreover, for many, Mao and Khomeini were fanatical tyrants, while others viewed them as successful revolutionaries who achieved great things for their peoples. Can one say legitimately that all these fanatics are powered by the same engine?

J. Glenn Gray[39] has proposed that the appeal of violence seems often connected with the increasing difficult of acting effectively in the modern world — that is, it is connected with powerlessness. The connection arises through a misunderstanding of power, especially in the political field. In it, power is often misunderstood as if it were a thing or element one could buy, store, and proffer when its use was deemed appropriate. But power, as Hannah Arendt has demonstrated, is merely potential, and as such it does not exist except while it is being actualized.[40] My power to convince, for example, exists only when my ability to speak convincingly is being actualized at the same time that my audience's ability to be convinced is also being actualized, so that my arguments are effective. But when this delicate balance of potential and actualization does not exist, there is a tendency to have recourse to force, and then to violence, so that one may safely assert that instances of violence are always proof that power has not been actualized; violence proves powerlessness. Powerlessness leads to frustration and impatience, passions that often overwhelm us; but, as the Greeks clearly understood, passions are something we undergo which reflect enslavement rather than freedom.

Recently Mark Lilla has argued that fanatical tyranny springs from an imbalance between reason and emotion.[41] Fanaticism, he maintains, arises when the *urge* toward an ideal grows unchecked by reason. Lilla points out that Plato had already identified as erotic (i.e., as based on Eros) the yearning for truth, for a certain social order, and for happiness. But precisely because it was an *urge*, a kind of madness, a reckless passion, it needed to be balanced by a healthy, reasonable perspective. The appetitive dimension of the psyche had to be checked by the rational dimension in order to achieve an orderly progress forward, both in the individual and in society at large. Failure to do so would inevitably result in an imbalance in the soul, a *dipsychia* whose outcome would be the one-sided passion of the fanatic.

Nietzsche had found a similar germ of fanaticism in the growth of the Dionysian without the counterbalancing development of the Apollonian[42] — in Freudian terms, in the cultivation of the Id at the expense of the Ego. Here, again, the fanatic emerges as a failed human being, one whose growth has been one-sided and out of sync.

But the phenomenon of fanaticism is so universal and widespread that other factors must be at work. Years ago Walter Kaufmann drew attention to a structure of decision avoidance which he termed *decidophobia* — really, the fear of leading an autonomous life.[43] Kaufmann noted how in matters of religion *decidophobia* (and, consequently, fanaticism) developed more easily because most of us are *born* into a religion whose tenets are inculcated in us from early childhood, thus making it very difficult to *choose* differently. The fear of choosing or of seriously considering alternatives is thus enhanced, and fanaticism arises as the predictable outcome. Even though convictions are prisons, as Nietzsche averred, the safety of the gaol often appears preferable to the uncertainty of questioning and the threatened danger of hell or excommunication.

James suggests that fanaticism may appear more readily in people whose minds are feeble and narrow, or in those whose character is masterful and aggressive. "A mind too narrow," he wrote, "has room but for one kind of affection. When the love of God takes possession of such a mind, it expels all human loves and human uses."[44] We see an example of this phenomenon in the single-mindedness with which some lovers attach themselves to each other, a fixation that all too often results in murders and suicides when thwarted.

There may also be a developmental factor here. Faith, like cognition and morality, grows through discernible stages, as the research of James Fowler has shown. Stage 3, Synthetic-Conventional faith, is characteristic of adolescence, but, as Fowler notes, all too often it becomes a permanent dwelling place: *"the dangers or deficiencies in this stage are twofold. The expectations and evaluations of others can be so compellingly internalized (and sacralized) that later autonomy of judgment and action can be jeopardized."*[45] Can we find in this stunted faith the roots of fanaticism?

Finally, one must note that fanaticism is a suicidal clutching, a not-letting-go. It is security desperate. Conversely, in a vibrant age, security is sin. "The instinct of self-preservation is suspended," wrote Nietzsche.[46] People squander themselves, pour themselves out in a generous outflow of talent, and they do this in the face of tragedy, even death, in order to involve themselves in the eternal joy of becoming.

These comments may not provide an exhaustive explanation of the roots of fanaticism, but they go a long way, I think, toward an adequate account of its endurance.

SCRIPTURES AND FANATICS

Many years ago, on the occasion of the celebration of the 850th anniversary of the birth of Maimonides, I presided over a session at a conference where several issues raised by Maimonides in his work came up for discussion by scholars. The afternoon was to close with a presentation by a renowned rabbi who was to summarize and critique the points made by the other speakers. The rabbi rose from his seat and walked to the podium. He opened a big tome to a preselected place, and pointing to a sentence, he read, "Maimonides is Torah, and we do not critique Torah." He closed the book, looked up at the audience, and said, "Gentlemen, I have other things to do. Good afternoon." And he strode out of the conference room.

In the same spirit, I have had students who were forbidden by their priests or rabbis to attend the classes where I discussed the Bible, for they believed that theirs was the only correct or orthodox interpretation.

Now, I believe that the text of the Hebrew Bible and the Christian Gospels and epistles is open to an ongoing study that has helped clarify the meaning of many passages and that is still being pursued, for, after all, new discoveries of scriptural texts and of cognate literatures continue to be made, and these need to be integrated into previous advances. The same goes for archaeological finds. While textual analysis is very important, I believe also that the results of historical and sociological research relevant to the texts in question add important — even crucial — elements to our understanding of the texts.[47] Thus, for instance, the translation of *Exodus* 13:18, "*yam-sûp*" as "Red Sea" (in the Septuagint and the Vulgate) is plainly wrong, since *sûp* means "reed" or "weed" (as in *Exodus* 2:3, 5: "bulrushes"); we should translate *yam-sûp* as "Reed Sea." A great deal of useless commentary and even experimentation, let alone dramatization, would have been avoided if the text had been properly translated. We have known this for a very long time, and yet priests and ministers continue to preach about the *Red* Sea, and movies continue to be made as if scholars had never written and as if translations were always infallible. But my concern here is not so much with the fidelity to the text as with the blind allegiance to it which is also at the root of fanaticism. Millions of people have no inkling into the complexities of translation or the predilections of translators (the Italians, aptly, spoke of translators as traitors — "*traddutore traditore*"), so they blindly follow a text simply because it is *there*.

Another example might be the recent discoveries of 900 B.C.E. inscriptions in Israel at Kuntillet ʿAjrud and at Khirbet el-Qôm in the Shephelah, in which YHWH is mentioned and depicted with a consort, "his Asherah" (the Canaanite Mother Goddess). This would indicate that the popular religion of the Hebrews at the time included the worship of male and female deities, YHWH and his Consort, not of the sole male God that the Bible projects. In fact, Berlinerblau has argued convincingly that the Bible may represent only a minority position among the Hebrews which became dominant, at least in writing, during the years following the return from the Babylonian Exile.[48] But how does one communicate such findings to a general populace thoroughly convinced that YHWH, and therefore the Christian God, was singularly male and alone, the only one in the area without a consort? And doesn't this blind belief, again, contain in itself the seeds of fanaticism?

FANATICISM AND HEROISM

In one of his essays, Schopenhauer wondered why we damn cowards and praise heroes who lose their lives for a great human cause. If self-preservation were the ruling passion, if it were a virtue, we should do the reverse, he thought, praise cowards and deem heroes foolish. So why the reverse?

The answer to this riddle, according to Schopenhauer, lies in the fact that, at times of great danger, we intuitively recognize the extension and continuation of our lives in the lives of others. In those sublime moments heroism is born. To the hero, the cessation of our individual lives is seen as the release of life from the fetters of individuality while it flickers unabated in billions of living beings. Life is not extinguished when we die: *we* are.[49]

Heroism is altruistic, but it is not fanatic. Fanatics remain bound by the strings of their own universalized principle, and, in altruistic suicide, they allow themselves to be overtaken by it. Even though their suicidal act is theirs, it is, rather, as if they were being overcome by something they had set in motion and are, now, unable to stop. Their stance is not truly willed; it is not truly voluntary (which is one reason why suicides are often excused on the grounds that they knew not what they were doing).

The hero, on the other hand, moves deliberately from one principle to another, higher one, from one "must" to another, higher "must." But this step is factual rather than principled. Both the fanatic and the hero face death, but the former is overcome by it, the latter endures it. The suicidal fanatic dies that the principle may live; the hero dies that people may live.

CONCLUSION: OVERVIEW

With profound insight, Ortega y Gasset commented that

all extremism inevitably fails because it consists in excluding, in denying all but a single point of the entire vital reality. But the rest of it, not ceasing to be real merely because we deny it, always comes back and back, and imposes itself on us whether we like it or not.[50]

Caligula found this at the end of his life when he concluded that his freedom, by which he played at being almighty God, was not the right one.[51] Caesar must have glimpsed this when he was stabbed to death by his own adopted son; and Napoleon Bonaparte must have meditated on this truth whiling his life away in exile on the island of St. Helena. We do not know, of course, nor do we know what crossed the mind of Savonarola when he was burned at the stake by the same townspeople he had inflamed with his extremist rhetoric, nor what flashed in the mind of Malcolm X when he was cut down by the same extremism he had spawned and then refused.

The truth, as all fanatics find out sooner or later, is that the whole world goes on living, loving, searching for happiness, while they pursue their puny dreams of grandeur in their postage-stamp-size quarter of the globe, and when the world finally notices them, it crushes them like an annoying gnat squashed between the pages of a book. In a way, blind faith, fanatical faith, is an exaggeration, a squandering of belief. It is grounded on the "all or nothing" position of a Father Paneloux who had given his all to God and therefore could have no friends, and would not call in a doctor when he was stricken with plague.[52]

To oppose fanaticism amounts to saying that there are no ultimate answers, and that to pretend there are, even in the name of God or country, is to deceive oneself. In an interview in 1948 Camus commented that "according to Pascal, error comes from exclusion,"[53] an idea he summarized in a lapidary statement, "Nothing is true that forces one to exclude."[54]

Another way of stating this is that the essence of right belief is moderation. As an Algerian, Camus was aware of the fact that in the tropics, at noon, the sun leaves no shadows. This was the image he chose to represent this thinking that rejects nothing and which keeps its eyes open to all the riches of the universe. He called it "thought at the meridian," or "noonday thought."[55] It may be the only real antidote to fanaticism.

... AND THE SCHOOLS

It may not be enough to identify the antidote to fanaticism in general, one may need to be specific about the ways to administer the remedy under penalty of being deemed too philosophical. It must be remembered that the publishers of the first Harry Potter novel did not think Americans would go for a book with the word "philosophy" in the title, so they changed it to *Harry Potter and the* Sorcerer's *Stone* from the original, *Harry Potter and the* Philosopher's *Stone* (emphasis added). With this change was lost, too, any allusion to the long history of the human quest for "The Philosopher's Stone."

At any rate, there are concrete things that can be done in the schools to prevent fanaticism. Many are obvious: help children clarify their values (and their parents' values!) by following the usual techniques of values clarification. This may entail, besides questioning, the exposure to the history and cultures of various peoples, including their religious traditions. But the clarification of values is not enough. It must be accompanied by a determined effort to teach children the love for the truth that alone can save us all. I have long been impressed by the fact that that bastion of Christian orthodoxy, St. Thomas Aquinas, used the arguments from Muslims, Jews, Greeks, and Romans to bolster his own search for truth. It is as if he were saying, "it makes no difference where the truth is found as long as it is found, just as it makes no difference where gold is found as long as it is gold."

There are many ways to instill in children this love for the truth. One way is exposure to the ways of truth in the various traditions and cultures of the world. This may be done by the introduction of folktales, myths, and other stories significant to the various cultures, for truth, as the Indians say of God, is one but wears many garbs. A Gujarati proverb has it that the Nameless sports many names. Rather than patronize other cultures from the point of view of our own, the point should be to learn to appreciate them all as purveyors of truth in the same way as we learn to value a diamond regardless of the diverse mountings it may be enshrined in.

A further point may be the learning of moderation. We live in a culture of exaggeration without regard for truth, where every new product is "the best," every building is "the tallest," every loan interest is "the lowest," every sweetener is "the sweetest," every flight "the fastest," and so on — all claims made without regard for truth. From this point of view, as Camus claimed, we live in a culture of lies, because to lie is not just to say what is not true but, equally, to claim more than is true.[56] We need to remind ourselves of the old Roman saying, "*modus in rebus*" ("moderation in all things") and of the Greeks' pursuit of "nothing in excess" which found individual happiness in the harmony and balance among all of the person's attributes and social happiness in the pursuit of justice.

In conclusion, if we want to prevent fanaticism and terrorism, we need to foster in children the feeling for the beauty and worth of human life, what Kant called "the beauty and dignity of human nature."[57] We achieve this by having schools in which respect for all the members of the community is warm and explicit, where teachers, pupils, parents, administrators, and staff treat each other with utmost care and consideration, so that such attitudes will become visceral in the children.

J. Glenn Gray has claimed that "A happy person will never — or almost never — give way to the destructive passions of rage and resentment. On the other hand, the unhappiness that arises from the frustration of action and consequently thwarted self-realization and deprivation of freedom is nearly bound to be violent."[58] The suggested corrective, besides creating conditions of empowerment and success, is taken from the work of Spinoza. In the *Ethics*,[59] Part 3, Spinoza maintains that if we imagine ourselves loving people, we will love them, and our subsequent actual love may destroy any hatred we may feel toward them. We make the latter action possible by means of the imagination. The imagination, in turn, is strengthened and made effective through action that, in a way, implements the affects we have imagined and entertained. Action may even give rise to the affects. Hence, as Aristotle had postulated,[60] it makes an enormous difference if we habituate children to act kindly, lovingly, respectfully, considerately, and truthfully, from their very youth, while supporting these actions with stories that exemplify them.

Jesus did this when he appropriated Hillel's lapidary summary of the Law, "Love God and love your neighbor," and explained what it meant to be a neighbor through a story. A traveler was set upon by robbers who left him for dead. A Priest came by, and then a Levite, too, and neither stopped to help. A Samaritan chanced by and he took care of the injured man. Then Jesus asked," Who was this man's neighbor?" "The one who showed him kindness," came the reply. Jesus added, "Go and do as he did."[61] St. Augustine understood what Jesus meant when he preached, "Love and do what you will,"[62] and sixteen hundred years later the Beatles sang about love being the only thing we need.

Similarly, according to a *hadīth*, one day a man came to visit the Prophet. When his name was announced, Mohammed muttered in disgust, "Oh, that shame of his clan it is, eh? That bad fellow?" But when he actually met the man, the Prophet was all smiles and dealt cheerfully with his visitor. After the man left, 'Ā'isha asked him to explain his behavior. Mohammed replied, "Why, 'Ā'isha, when have you seen me act grossly with people?"[63]

Finally, one must remember that the compassion of the Buddha Sakhyamuni is best exemplified in the *bodhisattva*, a seer who has attained enlightenment but at the last minute, in a sublime gesture of love, refuses release and returns to care for those who are still lost upon the way. Thus, in Kipling's novel, *Kim*, the Lama finally attains the freedom he had sought so assiduously. His soul goes free, soaring like an eagle, until he merges with the universal All. His mind is open to a thousand meditations in a thousand thousand years, passionless, aware of the Causes of all things. Suddenly, a voice cries out, "What shall come to the boy if thou art dead?" The Lama is shaken back and forth with pity for him, and he decides, "I will return to my *chela*, lest he miss the Way." And so he does. He pushes aside world upon world for his sake until he is once again squatting before him. "Son of my Soul," he says to Kim, "I have wrenched my Soul back from the Threshold of Freedom to free thee from all sin — as I am free, and sinless! Just is the Wheel! Certain is our deliverance! Come!"[64]

POSTSCRIPT

On the other hand, as Tevye used to say, there is another perspective. St. Augustine structured his *magnum opus, The City of God*, around two major concepts, that of a celestial city and that of an earthly city. "Two cities," he wrote "have been formed by two loves: the earthly by the love of self, even to the contempt of God: the heavenly by the love of God, even to the contempt os self."[65] By his own reckoning, the talk of "cities" is allegorical; he means two communities of people,[66] two realms, not geographic, but, rather, distinguished by different spiritual orientations, leading two distinct though parallel existences; and the citizens of each have similar aspirations, though what they mean by them, and what means they use to obtain them, differ considerably. For example, the earthly city desires peace, but its peace is purchased by war, and though peace in general is a good thing and worthy of pursuit, it remains precarious, since the vanquished are always likely to upset the victors and fight, in turn, for *their* peace.[67]

The heavenly peace, however, the peace of the eternal city — the heavenly Jerusalem; or Shambhala, in the Buddhist tradition — is indescribable and never to be lost once won. From this perspective, as Gur-Ze'ev points out,

> the division is not only . . . between a state of peace and a state of violence (or conflict), but in parallel also between *two essentially different states of peace*. (One could also say, between two different states of violences, one secular, the other sacred, yet called "peace.").[68]

The implication is that the earthly city's peace can eliminate fanaticism, violence, and terrorism only for a while, never eternally; and that by definition, the earthly city's peace is limited by the limitations of the city itself: it is grandiose, enervating, self-centered, profitable, endowed with a superficial wisdom, vain, and finally temporal, while the peace of the heavenly city defies description, though of it one can say, at least, that it is based on the transcendental wisdom and power of God. For in this other city, says St. Augustine, "there is no human wisdom, but only godliness, which offers due worship to the true God, and looks for its reward in the company of the saints, of holy angels as well as holy men and women, 'that God may be all in all.' "[69]

To say this is, of course, to claim that no earthly peace will be forever lasting; it is to assert that any elimination of fanaticism and terrorism can only be temporary, never enduring, and never perfect. Even if one denies the heavenly dimension of Augustine's argument, as many secularists do, still the historical evidence of the precariousness of all earthly achievements in this regard is overwhelming and gives witness to the truth of Augustine's perspective.

Freud, in his "Thoughts on War and Death" (1915),[70] made the case that the disillusionment experienced by all civilized people during World War I was based on the illusion that there could be perpetual peace and culture once people had reached a high level of civilization. But civilization is built on the control and/or suppression of powerful human instincts that are destructive in nature, and where the controls are flimsy, the façade is exposed as superficially strong and likely to collapse at the slightest provocation. Even if the controls are powerful and well coordinated, the instinctual forces may break through, especially where the masses are concerned. This is the nature of the state known as civilization, which can exist only at the expense of certain emotions and therefore is always on the brink of chaos, as a dam that is always near the point of collapse. No civilization can exist without its discontents.

Rabindranath Tagore expressed this idea of the basic imperfection of all earthly endeavors in beautiful language and imagery:

> When the creation was new and all the stars shone in their first splendour, the gods held their assembly in the sky and sang "Oh, the picture of perfection! The joy unalloyed!"
>
> But one cried of a sudden — "It seems that somewhere there is a break in the chain of light and one of the stars has been lost."
>
> The golden string of their harp snapped, their song stopped, and they cried in dismay — "Yes, that lost star was the best, she was the glory of all the heavens!"
>
> From that day the search is unceasing for her, and the cry goes on from one to the other that in her the world has lost its one joy!
>
> Only in the deepest silence of night the stars smile and whisper among themselves — "Vain is this seeking! Unbroken perfection is over all!"[1]

NOTES

1. William James, *The Varieties of Religious Experience* (New York: Mentor, 1964), p. 265.

2. Eric Hoffer, *The True Believer* (New York: Harper & Row, 1951).

3. Blaise Pascal, *Pensées* (New York: E. P. Dutton & Co., 1958), No. 100.

4. Max Scheler, *Ressentiment* (New York: Schocken Books, 1972).

5. Hoffer, *The True Believer*, pp. 80–81.

6. G. W. F. Hegel, *Phenomenology of Mind*, VI. B. III, "Absolute Freedom and Terror," in *Great Books of the Western World*, Robert M. Hutchins, ed. (Chicago: Encyclopedia Britannica, 1952), pp. 601–602.

7. J. Glenn Gray, *On Understanding Violence Philosophically and Other Essays* (New York: Harper Torchbooks, 1970), p. 22.

8. Richard M. Hare, *Freedom and Reason* (New York: Oxford University Press, 1965), p. 160. Also Marcus G. Singer, *Generalization in Ethics* (New York: Alfred A. Knopf, 1961).

9. Ibid., p. 178.

10. Herbert Marcuse, "Repressive Tolerance," in Robert Paul Wolff *et al.*, *A Critique of Pure Tolerance* (Boston: Beacon Press, 1969). Along similar lines, see Ilan Gur-Ze'ev, "Philosophy of Peace Education in a Postmodern Era," *Educational Theory* 51:3 (Summer 2001): 315-336.

11. Ibid., p. 90.

12. Catherine Weinberger-Thomas, *Ashes of Immortality: Widow-burning in India* (Chicago: The University of Chicago Press, 1999), p. 111.

13. Ibid., p. 20.

14. Ibid., p. 23.

15. Ibid., p. 29.

16. Ibid., p. 199.

17. Valmiki *Rāmāyana* 6.103.17 to 6.104.26 (Baroda: Oriental Institute, 1960-1975).

18. Weinberger-Thomas, *Ashes of Immortality*, p. 37.

19. Ibid., p. 134.

20. Emile Durkheim, *Suicide* (New York: The Free Press, 1951), p. 221.

21. Ibid., pp. 225-226.

22. See *Kālikā Purāna* 16:32-47.

23. Raghubir Singh Rathor, "Hamārī Samskriti aor Mahāsatyān," in *Mahāsatī Om Kanvar* (Jharli: Om Kanvar Trust, n.d.), pp. 8-12, quoted in Weinberger-Thomas, *Ashes of Immortality*, p. 174. Weinberger-Thomas herself writes: "It may be that the foreigners present a these scenes were attempting . . . to soften the shock of coming face to face with a form of otherness that appeared to them to be a repudiation of humanity itself" (p. 96).

24. The best study of the training of suicide bombers in Islam and of their religious convictions is Nasra Hassan, "An Arsenal of Believers," *The New Yorker*, November 19, 2001, pp. 36-41.

25. Paul Lehmann, *Ethics in a Christian Context* (New York: Harper & Row, 1963).

26. *1 Cor.* 2:10b-16; *Phil.* 2:6.

27. *The Passion of Saints Perpetua and Felicitas*, in *The Fathers of the Primitive Church*, Herbert A. Musurillo, ed. (New York: Mentor, 1966), p. 169. Also Joyce E. Salisbury, *Perpetua's Passion* (New York: Routledge, 1997).

28. Ibid., p. 171.

29. Eusebius, *Historia Ecclesiastica* 5.1.41.

30. Milton, *Samson Agonistes*, line 1665, in *Great Books of the Western World*, Robert M. Hutchins, ed. (Chicago: Encyclopaedia Britannica, 1952).

31. Jacques Maritain, *Man and the State* (Chicago: The University of Chicago Press, 1961), pp. 71-75. Also Primo Levi, *The Drowned and the Saved* (New York: Vintage, 1989), p. 75.

32. Maurice Merleau-Ponty, *Humanism and Terror* (Boston: Beacon Press, 1969), pp. xxxvi and 2.

33. Albert Camus, "The Renegade," in *Exile and the Kingdom* (New York: Vintage, 1958).

34. Albert Camus, "The Just Assassins," in *Caligula and Three Other Plays* (New York: Vintage, 1958).

35. Ibid., p. 258.

36. Che Guevara, "Man and Socialism in Cuba," in *Venceremos! The Speeches and Writings of Ernesto Che Guevara*, John Gerassi, ed. (New York: Simon & Schuster, 1968), p. 398.

37. Merleau-Ponty, *Humanism and Terror*, p. xxxvi.

38. Mohammed al-Ghazālī, *Ihya' 'ulum al-din* (6 vols.; Beirut: Dar al-Hadi, 1992), 3:14, in William C. Chittick and Sachiko Murata, *The Vision of Islam* (New York: Paragon House, 1994), p. 21.

39. J. Glenn Gray, *On Understanding Violence Philosophically and Other Essays* (New York: Harper Torchbooks, 1970).

40. Hannah Arendt, *The Human Condition* (New York: Doubleday Anchor, 1959), pp. 178-186.

41. Mark Lilla, "The Lure of Syracuse," *The New York Review of Books*, September 20, 2001.

42. Friedrich Nietzsche, *The Will to Power*, R. J. Hollingdale and Walter Kaufmann, transl. (New York: Random House, 1967).

43. Walter Kaufmann, *Without Guilt and Justice* (New York: Dell Publishing Co., Inc., 1973), p. 3.

44. James, *Varieties*, p. 267.

45. James W. Fowler, *Stages of Faith* (San Francisco: Harper & Row, 1981), p. 172. Emphasis in original.

46. Friedrich Nietzsche, *The Birth of Tragedy* (New York: Vintage, 1967).

47. For a somewhat different account, see Jack Miles, *Christ: A Crisis in the Life of God* (New York: Alfred A. Knopf, 2001), Appendix II, pp. 265-289.

48. Jacques Berlinerblau, "Official Religion and Popular Religion in Pre-Exilic Ancient Israel," <http://bibleinterp.com/articles/berlinerblau.htm> See also Amihai Mazar and Ephraim Stern, *Archaeology of the Land of the Bible* (New York: Doubleday, 1990 and 2001), Vol. 1, p. 447.

49. Arthur Schopenhauer, "On Ethics," in *Essays and Aphorisms*, R. J. Hollingdale, ed. (London: Penguin Books, 1970), pp. 140-141.

50. José Ortega y Gasset, *Man and Crisis* (New York: W. W. Norton & Co., 1962), p. 152.

51. Albert Camus, *Caligula and Three Other Plays*, p. 73.

52. Albert Camus, *The Plague* (New York: The Modern Library, 1948), pp. 206, 210.

53. Albert Camus, "Trois interviews," in *Essais*, Roger Quilliot, ed. (Paris: Éditions Gallimard, 1965), p. 379.

54. Albert Camus, "Return to Tipasa," in *Summer; Lyrical and Critical Essays*, Philip Thody, ed. (New York: Vintage, 1970), p. 165.

55. Albert Camus, "Helen's Exile," in *Summer; Lyrical and Critical Essays*, p. 153.

56. Albert Camus, "Preface to the American University edition of *The Stranger*" (1956), in *Lyrical and Critical Essays*, p. 336.

57. Immanuel Kant, *Beobachtungen über des Schönen und Erhabenen* [1764], in *Immanuel Kants Werke*, Ernst Cassirer, ed. (Berlin: Bruno Cassirer, 1922-1923), Vol. 2, p. 257.

58. J. Glenn Gray, *On Understanding Violence Philosophically*, p. 29.

59. Benedict de Spinoza, *Ethics*, in *Great Books of the Western World*, Robert M. Hutchins, ed. (Chicago: Encyclopedia Britannica, 1952).

60. Aristotle, *Nic. Ethics* II. 2 [1103ª 32–1103ᵇ 26].

61. *Luke* 10:25-37.

62. St. Augustine, *Tractatus VIII in Epistulam*; ML 35, 1978.

63. This *hadīth* is preserved by Al-Bukhārī in his *Kitāb al-Jāmi'al-Sahīh*, Krehl and Juynboll, eds. (Leyden, 1868-1908), Vol. IV, p. 121, in John Alden Williams, *Islam* (New York: George Braziller, 1962), p. 85. Some scholars do not consider Al-Bukhārī' collection to be fully reliable.

64. Rudyard Kipling, *Kim* (London: Macmillan & Co., Ltd., n. d.), pp. 411-413.

65. St. Augustine, *De Civ. Dei* XIV, 28, in *Great Books of the Western World*, Robert M. Hutchins, ed. (Chicago: Encyclopedia Britannica, 1952), p. 397.

66. Ibid., XV, 1, p. 398.

67. Ibid., XV, 4, p. 399.

68. Gur-Ze'ev, "Philosophy of Peace Education," p. 325.

69. St. Augustine, *De Civ. Dei* XIV, 28, p. 397. The quotation is from *1 Cor.* 15:28.

70. Sigmund Freud, "Thought on War and Death," in *Great Books of the Western World*, Robert M. Hutchins, ed. (Chicago: Encyclopedia Britannica, 1952).

71. Rabindranath Tagore, *Gitanjali* (London: Macmillan & Co., Ltd.,1966), #78, pp. 72-73.

6

The Structure of Humor

We need to keep in mind that the structure of faith is paradox. This chapter seeks to demonstrate that paradox is also the structure of humor. The reasons for belief and laughter, then, are fundamentally the same, and this may be one reason why the rictus on the Buddha's face is a sign of both the humor that attended his realization and the faith itself that was born with it.

HUMOR AND PARADOX

I explained in Chapter 1 how paradox is allergic to logic. It does not violate logic, but neither does it abide entirely by its dictates. This is why paradox can neither be proved right nor refuted; the possibility of its truth, however, is left open, perhaps to be decided at a higher level, in a new system. Gödel's formulations provide an example of what happens when systems become paradoxical: in their quest to be comprehensive their consistency is compromised, and so the data or propositions one sought to absorb in them become "undecidable," which, again, does not mean they are not true.

Faced with undecidable propositions or refractory data, one can intensify one's research until a breakthrough is achieved — the rat finds the hole in the wall of the barn and it escapes. It is possible, however, to look at the data, or the propositions, and simply pretend, just for fun, to put them together or to defuse their incompatibility with each other. This is what humor does. It takes two or more items that cannot be synthesized in the normal run of affairs, and rather than weep because of this, it creates an imaginary, make-believe exit accompanied by laughter.

The story is told that Zeno of Elea, fifth-century B.C.E. philosopher and follower of Parmenides, was once trying to prove to a small group of interested people that motion is impossible. He did this by means of paradoxes, several of which argued that, for motion to be possible, a moving object would have to traverse an infinite number of places in finite time, something which is impossible. He demonstrated this by drawing diagrams on the sand. As he looked up at his audience having finished his demonstration, they, too straightened up and walked away. Now, they could have stood there and argued with Zeno; they could have thought further about the problem and arrived at the distinction between infinite and indefinite; but they did nothing of the kind: they just got up and walked, probably with a smirk on their faces.

WHAT HUMOR IS

What is humor? Certainly, not every laughter. The laughter which is usually and naively associated with the comic is merely a physiological response to a number of diverse stimuli, only one of which is humor. As a physiological response, laughter can be triggered by a number of nonhumorous objects, actions, and situations. Thus laughter can be the result of tickling, or a release from nervous tension, or a reaction to unpleasant situations or events, or a way to put down danger or risk or unpleasant consequence ("laugh it off," we say), or the effect of inhaling nitrous oxide (appropriately called "laughing gas"). One can laugh for joy, for play, and for contests, but none of these laughters have to do necessarily with humor. "We often smile or laugh at things which are not comic," writes Max Eastman. "A smile, indeed, is our natural expression of welcome to anything we like, and a happy laugh is only a more thoroughgoing smile. It is necessary to distinguish this laugh of positive pleasure from the laugh that greets as comical a playful shock."[1]

The distinction between humorous and nonhumorous laughter is important not merely for the understanding of humor but also for the categorizing of animal laughter. Clearly, the fact of the similarity between human and animal laughter does not necessarily entail the conclusion that animals are humorous, any more than the fact of the physiological identity between humorous and nonhumorous laughter entails the conclusion that all laughter is humorous. Thus, on a scale from zero to ten, we have a continuum, from the zero of animal laughter — "the simple joy of living"[2] — and the one of nonhumorous laughter, to the ten of philosophical and theological laughter; from the laugh of the hyena and the satisfied gurgle of the human infant, to the laughter of Cervantes, Socrates, and the Buddha.

We are concerned here with humor, and with laughter only insofar as it is humorous. We want to inquire into the reasons why people laugh in a humorous way. Put differently, we want to look into the nature of humor. Several theories of humor have been proposed through the centuries, and even though it would be impossible to deal with all of them here in detail, a brief examination of their points of view is in order. I follow here the main lines of categorization developed by Monro in his excellent work, *Argument of Laughter*,[3] but my conclusions differ markedly from his own.

THEORIES OF HUMOR

Superiority Theories

Some of the earliest formulations of a theory of humor have sought to explain humorous laughter as a response to our perceived sense of *superiority* over others; or what comes to the same thing, as a response to our perception of the degradation of those around us. According to this point of view we laugh because we feel superior to others or see others as inferior to us.

Aristotle is credited with having been the first one to articulate this theory. In the *Poetics* he treated comedy as a special category of poetry. He saw comedy as being concerned with the laughable, which he defined as "a mistake or deformity not productive of pain or harm to others."[4] Ethical man that he was, he would not have considered it fit to laugh at the pain of others, or at what caused them harm. It was more a matter of laughing at their differences. In truth, we do not know what Aristotle's more refined view of humor was because the part of the *Poetics* which deals with comedy is lost.

Aristotle's point of view is echoed in Cicero's definition of humor as having its basis "on some kind or other of deformity or ugliness,"[5] or on things which have in them a trace of absurdity.[6] Many centuries later Hobbes maintained that laughter arises out of a sense of superiority, out of the spectacle of others' mistakes, defects, shortcomings, and so forth, especially when this apprehension of superiority is sudden or unexpected.[7]

Release Theories

Another set of theories see laughter, jokes, witticisms, and humor, generally, as a mode of *release* of psychological tensions. This is the view of L.W. Kline, J. C. Gregory, J. Kagan, A. Berlyne, G. Bateson, N. Frye, A. Wolfenstein, A. Grotjahn, and especially S. Freud.

For Freud, the essence of wit, the comic, and humor (Freud does make distinctions among these) depends on contrasting ideas,[8] on a comparison;[9] humor is a "Janus-like double-facedness."[10] He quotes Jean Paul's "Wit is the disguised priest who unites every couple," adding Vischer's postscript: "He likes best to unite those couples whose marriages the relatives refuse to sanction."[11] By this he means, of course, that wit brings together elements that normally are foreign or antithetical to each other and whose union, consequently, is not sanctioned by logic. Jean Paul's definition is listed: "Wit is the skill to combine with surprising quickness many ideas, which through inner content and connections are foreign to one another."[12]

However Freud, and the many psychologists who have followed him, is not so much concerned with the nature and definition of humor as with the mechanisms through which laughter is produced. For him this mechanism is to be found in the play of the unconscious. Therefore he is primarily concerned with the unconscious origin of the comic apprehension.

Freud saw at work in the comic the same mechanisms that operated in dreams — condensation, displacement, representation through absurdity or through the opposite, and so forth. He also saw the joke as the conscious externalization of material elaborated in the unconscious. Therefore jokes, like dreams, had to have manifest as well as latent content, which it was possible to elucidate through techniques similar to those of dream analysis. But while the mechanisms were similar in dream and in joke, and the purpose identical — pleasure — there was a major difference in mode, as it were: "The dream —," he wrote, "serves preponderantly to guard against pain, while wit serves to acquire pleasure."[13] Employing a distinction elaborated later, one can say that the dream is concerned with pleasure in a negative way (avoid pain) while the joke seeks pleasure positively. In effect, however, both mechanisms seek pleasure, though one overtly avoids pain (thereby protecting pleasure) and the other overtly seeks pleasure (thereby excluding pain).[14] Dreams and jokes achieve this by bringing together elements or dimensions of living whose union is not sanctioned by the ego.

In a later essay, "Humor" [1927], Freud wrote that "the essence of humor is that one spares oneself the effects to which the situation would naturally give rise and dismisses the possibility of such expressions of emotion with a jest."[15] In other words, "The ego refuses to be distressed by the provocations of reality, to let itself be compelled to suffer. It insists that it cannot be affected by the traumas of the external world; it shows, in fact, that such traumas are no more than occasions for it to gain pleasure."[16] Humor, that is, disarms the anxiety produced by disjunctions found in ordinary life; it treats them as evanescent, thereby generating laughter rather than tears. Thus "humor is not resigned; it is rebellious. It signifies not only the triumph of the ego but also of the pleasure principle."[17]

Humor requires the humorous attitude, which Freud says is "an attitude by means of which a person refuses to suffer, emphasizes the invincibility of his ego by the real world, [and] victoriously maintains the pleasure principle."[18] As such, then, humor is preliminary to the joke, which Freud always saw as a reflection of the unconscious. Essentially, humor is a transfer of energy by the Ego to the Superego, which then can take toward the Ego the attitude of a parent toward a child: "Don't worry; it's OK." "To the Superego, thus inflated, the Ego can appear tiny and all its interests trivial."[19] In brief, humor is *the contribution made to the comic through the agency of the superego.*[20]

Freud obviously acknowledges the disjunction that occasions laughter, and he is aware of the incompatibility of the logics of each alternative. The jokes he tells and the analyses he makes all give evidence of this understanding. But Freud is not interested in an analysis of the structure of the joke *per se* or as it is humorous, but, rather, in what the disjunction reveals about the person's unconscious and the divergent tendencies within it. A few examples may clarify this distinction.

> A psychology professor is lecturing to his class when a rather voluptuous young woman sitting in the front row sneezes loudly. "Breast you!" says the professor, hardly altering the rhythm of his presentation.

We laugh at the junction of "breast" and "bless," but Freud would want to know what the substitution of "breast" for "bless" signifies — whether it reveals a preoccupation with female anatomy, an incipient sexual attraction, or simply nothing at all. Freud, in other words, would *use* the joke as he would *use* a dream, as a tool for analysis of the unconscious. However, not all jokes, witticisms, or comic situations arise necessarily out of unconscious conflicts.

The story is told that Erik Erikson was once lecturing at Harvard University on the unconscious substitutions for masturbation, among which he mentioned knitting. A young woman who was sitting in the front row, and who was quietly knitting a shawl, is said to have quipped, "Professor Erikson, masturbation is masturbation and knitting is knitting."

Years ago I was lecturing on the Marxist notion of "species-life." I had prepared my class thoroughly, anticipating questions and bringing to class books that would lend authority to my answers. As I had foreseen, the question was asked, "And what about sex?" "I am glad you asked this questions about sex," I said as I looked into my book bag, ready to proffer the appropriate book, and realized, to my consternation, that I had not brought the volume to class. "I didn't bring mine to class today," I said, as the students burst into laughter.

Instances like these probably do not reveal any serious unconscious conflicts about sexuality. At any rate, they can be enjoyed purely for their humorous content, leaving the analysis thereof to the psychologists.

I should add that in so far as Freud recognizes the origin of humor in the disjunction of events or circumstances, his views might be better classified among the incongruity theories.

Ambivalence Theories

A third theory makes humor hinge on *ambivalence*. This theory, which can claim few adherents (among them J. Y. T. Greig and V. K. Krishna Menon), maintains that laughter is essentially a subjective response to the experience of conflicting attitudes and emotions. As such, it is probably best subsumed under incongruity theories. It represents a weaker statement, as it were, of incongruity theories.

Incongruity Theories

Finally, *incongruity* theories maintain that humor (and the accompanying laughter) arises out of perceived incongruity or paradox. "Humor," says Pirandello, "consists of the feeling of the opposite produced by the special activity of reflection."[21] It is this theory that, in my own estimation, most clearly accounts for the nature of humor. In truth, it seems to me that it encompasses all the other theories insofar as incongruity is essentially present in all of them, a fact easy to demonstrate. After all, the apprehension of superiority involves relationally the incongruity between superior and inferior, and the tension that is released in witticism is that between desire and reality. Incongruity thus seems to be at the root of all humorous situations. It is the true trigger of humorous laughter.

James Beattie, in "An Essay on Laughter and Ludicrous Composition" (1764),[22] remarked perceptively how "certain forms of irregularity and unsuitableness raise within us that agreeable emotion whereof laughter is the outward sign."[23] And even though not all incongruous combinations necessarily lead to laughter, he believed the reverse to be invariably true: "Every ludicrous combination is incongruous."[24]

Beattie's definition follows: "Laughter arises from the view of two or more objects or ideas, disposing the mind to form a comparison."[25] He interpreted both Aristotle and Hobbes accordingly (as I have suggested above), and went on to insist that it is not mere comparison that is at the root of humorous laughter, but real inconsistency, incongruity, and paradox. Laughter, he concluded, "arises from the view of two or more inconsistent, unsuitable, or incongruous parts or circumstances, considered as united in one complex object or assemblage, or as acquiring a sort of mutual relation from the peculiar manner in which the mind takes notice of them."[26]

Schopenhauer took essentially the same position. For him "*laughter* results from nothing but the suddenly perceived incongruity between a concept and the real objects."[27] Again: "The origin of the ludicrous is always the paradoxical, and thus unexpected, subsumption of an object under a concept that is in other respects heterogeneous to it."

I would submit that incongruity theories are the ones that most closely describe the origin of humor. It should be clear, then, that incongruity and paradox may be deemed to be at the root of humor, though the relationship between paradox and humor has not been fully developed as yet. This relationship will be explored in the writings of the following theoreticians.

KIERKEGAARD, BERGSON, KOESTLER

It is in the writings of Kierkegaard, Bergson, and Koestler that one encounters a more thorough and profound explanation of the relation between paradox and humorous laughter. For Kierkegaard , "what lies at the root of the comic . . . is the discrepancy, the contradiction";[28] the comical "is always rooted in the contradictory."[29] Humor, for him, is a universal experience because "where there is life there is contradiction, and wherever there is contradiction, the comical is present."[30] Thus for Kierkegaard the universality of laughter is to be explained in terms of its association with the absurd, which is itself ubiquitous. Besides stating and developing the relation between absurdity and humor, Kierkegaard contributes a profound understanding of the humor attitude, of which more will be said later.

For Bergson, humor arises out of contradiction. Here it is the opposition between what he calls mechanical inelasticity and living pliableness that constitutes the laughable.[31] But Bergson's is no mere repetition of the relation between humor and paradox. What triggers humorous laughter, he says, is the fact that the incongruous elements coming together are not usually experienced or perceived as being compatible. Bergson writes: "A situation is invariably comic when it belongs simultaneously to two altogether independent series of events and is capable of being interpreted in two entirely different meanings at the same time."[32]

It is Koestler, however, who develops the notion of incongruity as the origin of humor in the most systematic and clear manner. His theory of humor is well known. It is a primary example and part of his theory of insight. The key term is *bisociation*. According to Koestler, an insight occurs whenever two previously unrelated events, ideas, theories, or systems intersect at one point. In Koestler's words, insight is *"the perceiving of a situation or idea . . . in two self-consistent but habitually incompatible frames of reference. . . .* The event . . . in which the two intersect, is made to vibrate simultaneously on two different wavelengths, as it were. While this unusual situation lasts . . . [the event] is not merely linked to one associative context, but *bisociated* by two."[33]

As an example of this bisociation in humor, Koestler cites a number of jokes. I take one he borrows from Freud, who in turn borrows it from Chamfort.

> The story concerns a Marquis at the court of Louis XIV who, on entering his wife's boudoir and finding her in the arms of a Bishop, walked calmly to the window and went through the motions of blessing the people in the street.
> "What are you doing,?" cried the anguished wife.
> "Monseigneur is performing my functions," replied the Marquis, "so I am performing his."[34]

Koestler explains. Here, as in many jokes, "two implicit codes of behavior are brought into collision"[35]: the code involving the rules of celibacy, which forbids bishops sexual behavior as well as any dalliance, and the code involving the rights and duties, sexual and otherwise, of a married layman. In the confrontation of codes, the bishop engages in sexual behavior — which is forbidden him but allowed to the marquis — and in the resolution the marquis blesses the crowds — which is forbidden him but permitted to the bishop. It is this reversal of function in the resolution that produces the explosion of laughter.

One must note further, as Koestler does, that "the crucial point about the Marquis's behavior is that it is unexpected and perfectly logical — but of a logic not usually applied to this type of situation."[36] The usual logic would require the acknowledgment by the bishop of his behavior in violation of his code, and of his consequent sinfulness, requiring confession and expiation. But this is not what takes place here. Instead, there is a jump to another logical plane, one in which the roles are reversed with impunity. This is the logic of humor. According to Koestler, therefore, the conditions that obtain in the moment of humor are:

1. the presence of independent planes, codes, or systems,
2. which are logically consistent within themselves, and also self-sufficient as far as they go,
3. but which are suddenly bisociated in one trans-systemic moment.

Making use of the concepts and terms introduced at the beginning of this study, I may restate the conditions in the following manner. As systems go, and given certain presuppositions, the code of celibacy is logically consistent and self-sufficient. So is the code of the layman. In the normal run of affairs, the bishop's behavior and the marquis's conduct are governed by their respective codes, and violations are treated according to the specific measures formulated in the respective codes. What we have in the joke is the paradoxical situation of role reversal *as a solution to a violation of the bishop's code.* This solution is not acceptable within the logic of either code. What makes the joke is an appeal to this "new" system or code in which reversal *is* possible. It is in the singularity of this appeal to a higher system that both established codes momentarily become bisociated in humor.

The predicament of the bishop is a paradoxical one, in a strictly logical meaning of the term. Celibacy and adultery are logically self-exclusive. If the Bishop is celibate, how come he is in the arms of the marquis's wife? Rendering the situation into logical terms, we have two statements, "bishop is celibate" (A), and "bishop is not celibate" (~A), both of which cannot be true within the same system if the system is to be consistent. According to Koestler, however, the paradox is "solved" by a move to a different logic, that of an "as if " system envisioned purely for the sake of an exit. This is humor. The paradox created by the self-contradictory statements "bishop is celibate" and "bishop is not celibate" is escaped by means of Gödel's first theorem: the statement "bishop is not celibate" is true (factually) but (logically) unprovable within the system. The moment this is realized, the possibility exists of creating an evanescent, momentary solution to the paradox *outside the logic of the celibacy code*; that is, in the higher system. of the joke. Reversibility of function is the actual means for this trans-systemic solution.

THE HUMOR ATTITUDE

The case has been made so far that incongruity is at the root of humor. Humorous laughter, therefore, cannot deserve this categorization except in the presence of paradox.[37] But the question may be asked whether or not perceived incongruity, though a *necessary* condition, is also a *sufficient* condition of humor. The answer is No. Clearly, perceived incongruity may lead to a number of outcomes that have nothing to do with humor. Thus, for instance, paradox may lead to fear, despair, bewilderment, or curiosity.[38]

If paradox is a necessary but not a sufficient condition of humor, we must search for the element that decisively differentiates between the humorous and the nonhumorous apprehension of paradox. This element is *the humorous attitude*. One may say that while paradox is necessary *a parte objecti*, it alone does not suffice. The humorous attitude must supervene *a parte subiecti* in order for the perception to eventuate in laughter. In what does the humor attitude, the sense of humor, consist? The work of Kant may give us some idea of its nature.

For Kant, humor was a talent, "the talent for being able to put oneself at will into a certain frame of mind in which everything is estimated on lines that go quite off the beaten track (a topsy-turvy view of things) and yet on lines that follow certain principles."[39] In other words, humor depends on the talent, the capacity to transport oneself beyond self-repelling systems to a new system where unheard of solutions are possible. What is this talent? It is the imagination, which is "a powerful agent for creating, as it were, a second nature out of the material supplied to it by actual nature. It affords us entertainment where experience proves too commonplace."[40] The imagination, therefore, is the root of the sense of humor.

The result is a form of play (*Gedankenspiel*), the game of jest. This game consists in presenting to the understanding something other than expected. As a result, when the understanding is confronted with an outcome, interpretation, or what have you, different from what it expected, it lets go. The bodily tension that had accumulated as the understanding moved towards the expected rational climax of the event is suddenly released in the new unexpected way, and physicomental equilibrium is regained. This release is laughter, *"an affection arising from a strained expectation being suddenly reduced to nothing."*[41]

The fact that the expectations built by the understanding as it pursues its course toward a rational solution are thwarted, cannot be the cause of laughter, says Kant. If anything, they would be the cause for disappointment. What constitutes humor, then, is an imaginative passage to the realm of play — of the specific game of jesting: "the bubble of our expectation was extended to the full and suddenly went off into nothing."[42] This nothing is the realm of play, into which we pass momentarily until equilibrium is regained following the convulsion of laughter. The joke is the momentary step from the realm of the serious and the logical to that of play, accompanied by tension-reducing laughter, and followed by a return to the serious realm of logic.

Thus, according to Kant, the sense of humor is constituted by the playful attitude. This seems to be an insightful explanation of it. Says Eastman: "Humor is play. Humor is being in fun. It has no general value except the values possessed by play."[43] Again: "It is necessary to be, or become, playful in order to perceive anything whatever as funny."[44] In Piagetian terms, the sense of humor hinges on the capacity to be more assimilative than accommodative, more subjective than objective. Put differently, it consists in the capacity to turn from the accommodative and objective to the subjective and assimilative, from seriousness to play. Plato had already seen the serious and the humorous as sisters,[45] and Aristotle had considered the ability to turn properly from seriousness to humor as a highly desirable human characteristic. For him, to be an *eutrapelos anthropos* (*homo bene vertens*) — a person with a ready wit, we might say — was an immensely worthwhile ideal.[46]

We have seen Kant suggest that the humorous attitude is a passage into *nothing*. Kierkegaard specifies this further by indicating that the humorous attitude characteristically sees the paradox as canceled — in other words, "as if " it did not exist, or "as if " it had been turned to naught. Not that the paradox is made to disappear logically, as if a solution had been found: "the comical does not indeed cancel the contradiction, but a legitimate comic apprehension can do so"[47] momentarily. That is, for an instant, in the joke, the paradox is experienced "as if" it were canceled, even though in fact it is not. The trans-systemic leap, in other words, is of short duration; it is temporary, not permanent.

Put differently, the humorous attitude, insofar as it is a playful attitude, is capable of achieving what all playful attitudes do: it can superimpose one reality on another without destroying the latter. Thus one becomes a player in a game without ceasing to be who one is in the serious world of work; or one becomes an actor in a play without ceasing to be oneself. Similarly, the sense of humor does not obliterate the reality of the paradox that gives it birth; merely it overlays it with laughter.

Only the human imagination is capable of effecting this illusory and momentary cancellation of the paradox. It is the imagination that renders the human mind capable of seeing resolution, exit, escape, where the objective apprehension sees only the roadblock of paradox.

CONCLUSION

"Humor" comes from the Latin word meaning moisture (Greek *hygros*), and referred at one time to the fluids within us which, it was thought, made us phlegmatic, choleric, sanguine, or melancholic. The word, therefore, carried the connotation of something physiological, something bodily. To speak of a "sense of humor," one might say, implies that it is like nature to those who have it, or like second nature to those who have acquired it.

What sparks this sense of humor is the ludicrous, that is, the playful (Latin *ludus* means "play"). In all of this, as can be seen, etymology confirms what was said above. For play itself is a mysterious activity that superimposes itself on the ordinary without destroying it.

NOTES

1. Max Eastman, *Enjoyment of Laughter* (New York: Simon & Schuster, 1936), p. 11.

2. Joaquín Gabaldón Márques and Antonio José Anzola-Carrillo, *La risa de Sócrates y otras risas* (Buenos Aires: Imprenta López, 1962), p. 92.

3. David H. Monro, *Argument of Laughter* (Notre Dame, IN: University of Notre Dame Press, 1963). An excellent summary may be found in John Allen Paulos, *Mathematics and Humor* (Chicago: The University of Chicago Press, 1980), Chapter 1.

4. Aristotle, *Poetics* 5 [1448ª 32-36].

5. Cicero, *De Orat.*, II, 58, in *Oeuvres Complètes* (Paris: Firmin-Didot, 1881).

6. Ibid., II, 71.

7. Hobbes, *Leviathan* I, 6, in *Great Books of the Western World*, Robert M. Hutchins, ed. (Chicago: Encyclopaedia Britannica, 1952). See Lawrence La Fave, Jay Haddad, and William A. Maesen, "Superiority, Enhanced Self-esteem, and Perceived Incongruity Humor Theory," in *Humor and Laughter: Theory, Research, and Application*, Tony Chapman and Hugh Foot, eds. (London: J. Wiley & Sons, 1976), pp. 64-65.

8. Sigmund Freud, *Wit and its Relation to the Unconscious*, in *The Basic Writings of Sigmund Freud*, A. A. Brill, ed. (New York: The Modern Library, 1938), p. 789.

9. Ibid., p. 795.

10. Ibid., p. 803.

11. Ibid., pp. 634-635.

12. Ibid., p. 635.

13. Ibid., p. 761.

14. Ernst Kris, "Ego Development and the Comic," *International Journal of Psychoanalysis* 19 (1938): 77-90. Also Paul McGhee, "Development of the Humor Response," *Psychological Bulletin* 76:5 (1971): 328-348.

15. Sigmund Freud, *Collected Works*, Standard Edition, James Strachey, ed. (London: Hogarth Press, 1961), Vol. 21, p. 162.

16. Ibid., p. 162.

17. Ibid., p. 163.

18. Ibid.

19. Ibid., p. 164.

20. Ibid., p. 165.

21. Luigi Pirandello, *On Humor* (Chapel Hill, NC: University of North Carolina Press, 1974), p. 145.

22. James Beattie, *Essays* (Edinburgh: William Greech, 1776).

23. Ibid., p. 585.

24. Ibid., p. 605.

25. Ibid., p. 601.

26. Ibid., p. 602.

27. Arthur Schopenhauer, *The World as Will and Representation* (Indian Hills, CO: The Falcon's Wing Press, 1958), Vol. I, #13, p. 59.

28. Kierkegaard, *Concluding Unscientific Postscript* (Princeton, NJ: Princeton University Press, 1968),, pp. 82-83.

29. Ibid., p. 378.

30. Ibid., p. 459.

31. Henri Bergson, "Laughter," in *Comedy*, Wylie Sypher, ed. (New York: Doubleday Anchor, 1956), pp. 66-67, 84.

32. Ibid., p. 123.

33. Arthur Koestler, *The Act of Creation* (New York: Macmillan, 1964), p. 35.

34. Ibid., p. 33.

35. Ibid., p. 84.

36. Ibid., p. 35.

37. Göram Herhardt, "Incongruity and Funniness: Toward a New Descriptive Model," in *Humor and Laughter*, Chapman and Foot, eds., p. 55.

38. Mary K. Rothbart, "Incongruity, Problem-solving, and Laughter," in *Humor and Laughter*, Chapman and Foot, eds., p. 38. Also La Fave, Haddad, and Maesen, "Superiority, Enhanced Self-esteem, and Perceived Incongruity Humor Theory," p. 86, and Thomas R. Shultz, "A Cognitive-developmental Analysis of Humor," in *Humor and Laughter*, Chapman and Foot, eds., p. 12.

39. Immanuel Kant, *Critique of Judgment*, Part I, Section I, Book II, B, § 54, in *Great Books of the Western World*, Robert M. Hutchins, ed. (Chicago: Encyclopaedia Britannica, 1952), Vol. 42, p. 539.

40. Ibid., § 49, pp. 528-529.

41. Ibid., § 54, p. 538.

42. Ibid.

43. Eastman, *Enjoyment of Laughter*, p. 15.

44. Ibid.

45. Plato, *Philebus* 50B and *Epistle VI* 323D.

46. Aristotle, *Nic. Ethics* IV, 8 [1128 [a]]. Xenophon, *Cyropaedia*, G. Gemoll, ed. (Cambridge: Oxford University Press, 1912), VI, 1, 6 and VIII, 3, 4. Also Aquinas, *In decem libros ethicorum Aristotelis ad Nichomacum*, in *Opera Omnia*, E. Fretté and P. Maré, eds. (Paris: 1872-1880), Lib. IV, lect. 16.

47. Kierkegaard, *Concluding Unscientific Postscript*, p. 466.

7

On Frivolity

There is perhaps no worse enemy of humor than frivolity. Frivolity is that quality of life or turn of mind that makes us go for the easy and the pleasant, the superficial and even the vulgar, rather than the deep and the paradoxical. The rationale is easy to find: why bother with difficult stuff, classical music and literature, risk and danger, when there is no financial profit or fame in it? Why strive to be the best when the mediocre get paid the same, or even more?

Years ago, in an insightful and deeply troubling book, Elaine Kendall commented how Americans seem to be "in full flight from a personal esthetic, from any commitment to style. Somehow freedom of choice has finally led us to seek freedom *from* choice," she wrote. "We have found a way to eat, to dress ourselves, and live without making any real decisions."[1] The result is the mediocrity of the food most of us consume, the dress most of us wear, the ideas most of us live by, and the humor most of us enjoy, so-called soaps and sitcoms.

There is no real humor at the base of most of our entertainment, but just a vapid, tepid sort of pabulum that is very difficult to describe. The most that can be said of it is that it makes money, which seems to be the only yardstick of success.

Tolstoy, in *War and Peace*, describes a party at Speránski's, a popular and powerful political leader at the time, in which the purpose seemed to be to amuse the host and prevent him from thinking about anything serious, especially political. Therefore all kinds of jokes, declamations, and gossips that might prove funny, were engaged in, but the result seemed to be somewhat empty and inconsequential. Tolstoy comments, "There was nothing wrong or unseemly in what they said, it was witty and might have been funny, but it lacked just that something which is the salt of mirth, and they were not even aware that such a thing existed."[2] The party, in other words, had been a frivolous affair, and the participants, to judge by their attitude when their host absented himself, themselves had an inkling of it, though they had participated willingly and, if asked, would have probably replied that they had enjoyed themselves, that they had had "fun." One must be reminded, however, that God, according to *Revelation* 3:16, sent this message to the people of Laodicea:

"Because you are lukewarm, neither hot nor cold, I will vomit you out of my mouth"; that is, "your frivolity makes me puke!"

THE REVOLT OF THE FRIVOLOUS

Frivolity would be a minor problem in society, a small anomaly barely noticed in social analyses, were it not for the fact that the common person, the frivolous person, has become the norm, its numbers having increased exponentially in recent times. This rise in numbers Ortega y Gasset labeled "the revolt of the masses." By "mass" Ortega did not have in mind a certain social class of people, but, rather, a type of person to be found in all social strata; moreover, "mass" had nothing to do with economic conditions: it did not stand for the poor or dispossessed, but for a certain character that, again, was found at all levels of society, but, significantly in our modern world, in greater numbers than ever before.[3]

"Mass" (in Spanish *masa*) means, obviously, great numbers, but it also means "dough," and perhaps it means great numbers because it means dough: "mass" is malleable, as if one were saying that "mass" represents the great numbers of people who can be kneaded like dough. "Mass," like "dough," also has the connotation of shapelessness, of undifferentiation: a bit of dough can be turned into bread of any number of shapes. Thus, "mass" means people as undifferentiated from each other[4] and therefore as average, or as quantifiable into averages: "mass" designates what is average among people, not what is distinctive, peculiar, even extravagant. "Mass" is the common denominator. Now, what is special in our times, says Ortega, is that this type of human being, having grown in numbers and drawing strength from numbers, asserts itself and its ordinariness to the point of excluding what is excellent in every field: *"the characteristic of the hour is that the commonplace mind, knowing itself to be commonplace, has the assurance to proclaim the rights of the commonplace and to impose them wherever it will."* [5] We live, in other words, as Elaine Kendal saw it, in the era of the rights of the mediocre, where to be different is to be indecent. The result, according to Ortega, is that most people today

> are *uncultured*: they are ignorant of the essential system of ideas concerning the world and man, which belong to our time. This average person is the new barbarian, a laggard behind the contemporary civilization, archaic and primitive in contrast with his problems, which are grimly, relentlessly modern. This new barbarian is above all the professional man, more learned than ever before, but at the same time more uncultured — the engineer, the physician, the lawyer, the scientist[6]

— to which one should add the teacher, the businessperson, and the politician. The modern professional is a specialist; that is, a person who knows a lot about very little and very little about a lot.[7] For the specialists consciousness is fixed, awareness is petrified, but they "know" a lot. Their selves are real only insofar as they are useful to the particular industry for which they were trained, and they can be discarded like so much dead weight the moment the data base changes or contracts — this is why lay-offs occur in large numbers at one time; they are trimmed just as a superfluous piece of dough is trimmed from a loaf of bread, or a cookie, or a pie crust.

In one of his early books, *Schopenhauer as Educator* (1874), Nietzsche remarked that the distinguishing characteristic of people in his time — and it continues to be in ours — was inertia, a certain idleness caused by the fear of going against the current of public opinion which demands convention and hides behind it.[8] "Public opinion," says Nietzsche, "is private inertia."[9] A case in point is the public opinion poll, to which we are so drawn precisely because it saves us a lot of individual effort. Polls are merely the statistical standardization of the majority opinion *without the reasons for the opinion*, the implication being, of course, that in the case of the masses, their reasons do not matter at all, since these are, after all, the reasons of "the masses." Polls have usefulness in certain, very limited, conditions; but to use them as widely as they are currently used is surely indicative of the fact that they dispense with the painstaking approach to opinion which involves discussion, argument, and the formation of conscience.

The blurting out of opinions without the consideration of the reasons behind them turns the opinions into utterances whose significance is reduced to a mere numerical quotient devoid of all personality. But a frivolous culture does not even notice this, excited at the fact of having been asked its opinion. Like Mildred Montag, Guy Montag's wife in Ray Bradbury's *Fahrenheit 451*, who has been given a role in an interactive TV play, which she describes to her husband:

> "They write the script with one part missing. It's a new idea. The homemaker, that's me, is the missing part. When it comes time for the missing lines, they all look at me out of the three walls and I say the lines. Here, for instance, the man says, 'What do you think of this whole idea, Helen?' And he looks at me sitting here center stage, see? And I say, I say —" She paused and ran her finger under a line on the script. " 'I think that's fine!' And then they go on with the play. . . . Isn't that fun, Guy?"[10]

And most of us think it is fun to be asked for our opinion even though an opinion without reasons for it is a disembodied utterance that, in the statistical process to which it will be subjected, will be further depersonalized and turned into a collective number.

In such a mass environment frivolity reigns supreme, and it is almost impossible to withstand its impact and laugh only with those who have seen through to their own inner selves and who, to know who they really are, ask themselves, "What have you really laughed at in your life? What has dominated your soul and made it happy?"[11]

THE FEUILLETON

Frivolity manifests itself in many ways, one of which is the popular press. In his *opus magnum*, *The Glass Bead Game*, which takes place hundreds of years in the future, Hermann Hesse described our present age as "the Age of the Feuilleton" (*folleto*, in Spanish), that is, the age of the feature article contained in loose inserts or sections added to the newspapers (French *feuille* means leaf or sheet of paper).

The historian who narrates the events in the novel admits to having difficulty defining a "feuilleton," but he hazards the following description: "They [the Feuilletons] seem to have formed an uncommonly popular section of the daily newspapers, were produced by the millions, and were a major source of mental pabulum for the reader in want of culture."[12] And he added:

> The Age of the Feuilleton was by no means uncultured; it was not even intellectually impoverished. But [it] . . . appears to have had only the dimmest notion of what to do with culture. Or rather, it did not know how to assign culture its proper place within the economy of life and the nation.[13]

Hesse probably took as his model the *feuilleton* which became popular in Vienna at the end of the nineteenth century. To the feuilletonist, culture became the subjective feeling of culture. How one felt became synonymous with how one thought: our popular language still reflects this narcissistic attitude, and we often attribute to personal feelings an unquestioning finality we deny to objective events. Thus we presume that art and movie critics only give us their feelings about the pieces they critique, and we respond by saying that our feelings are as good a measure as theirs, ignoring, of course, the reasoning behind the critiques, and confusing once more valuing with evaluating.[14]

Today, corresponding to these pseudocultural inserts, is the so-called comic page, a section similarly devoted to humor to which millions turn daily in order to get their laughs. The problem is not with the comics themselves: their humor is often extraordinarily clever and entertaining. The problem is that for most people this is the only kind of humor they are exposed to, the only humor that feeds their sensibilities, the humor they judge other humor by, therefore leaving unrecognized and unacknowledged and unenjoyed the quintessential forms of humor in Don Quixote, Falstaff, Peer Gynt, Brer Rabbit, Buddha, Malvolio, Eliza Doolittle, Harry Haller, Loki, and countless others whose humor is not featured in the comics pages, and not because they are not funny! As Elaine Kendall would say, of all the riches of humor available to us, we have become satisfied with the least funny, the superficial, the trivial, the frivolous.

UNDERACHIEVERS

The story is told of a college student who fell asleep during his Middle English class. The professor, angry at this display of inattention, hurled a book at him. The book missed its target, but the noise of its impact awoke the student who asked a classmate, "What was *that* ?" The class mate replied, "A flying Chaucer."

This joke could have been a typical incident in the life of William, the protagonist of Benjamin Anastas's novel, *An Underachiever's Diary*.[15] William, an intellectually gifted young man, cruises through the early decades of his life like a ship through a series of ocean reefs, scraping here and there against the coral without ever foundering altogether. William is a self-made underachiever. Among his few accomplishments is a detailed document on underachievement, a kind of manifesto for those who would rather switch than fight — not that they cannot fight, but they simply do not. Underachievers, according to William, long for inclusion while despising every group; neither optimists nor pessimists, they merely decline to play; "entrusted with a master key to opportunity's home office,"[16] they misplace it.

William's rationale for this state of affairs is that no one is ever finished, "we are a litany of criminals against perfection that will last forever, or at least until our time on this spinning puddle comes to an end";[17] but this argument rings hollow. He seems to say that, because we cannot be perfect, we should not even try; but one could just as easily argue the reverse: because we cannot be perfect, we *must* strive, even if the reward is nothing but the struggle itself. Such was the advice of old Peleus to his son Achilles: to strive always among the best, and to keep ahead of all peers.[18] It is our satisfaction with mediocrity that allows us to underachieve in the primary areas of culture and to be content with news and gossip[19] while we could be laughing the godlike laughter of the Immortals, as Hesse called them.[20]

Some of our frivolity is caused by our misconception of democracy; or, rather, by the misapplication of this term to areas where it is totally inappropriate. Democracy is a form of government, not a method of inquiry nor a yardstick of truth: truth is not determined by majority vote, nor are moral good and evil.

Before he died, C. S. Lewis added to his popular book, *The Screwtape Letters*, a speech supposedly delivered by Screwtape at his retirement party. In it, Screwtape counseled the audience of devils to use the word "democracy" as an incantation, as a slogan designed to settle any kind of argument where the pursuit of perfection might be at stake. To try to speak well, both with regard to pronunciation and with regard to grammar and style; to listen to good music, both popular and classic; to read good literature, especially the true and tried classics, would make one stand out, be different, be ahead of one's peers — therefore it must be undemocratic![21]

The result is not merely that the frivolous feel fully justified in not striving after excellence, but that the excellent feel uncomfortable in their pursuit, especially if the charge of elitism is hurled at them, as if it were ever a bad thing to strive after perfection. In this manner the mediocre bask in their mediocrity while subtly dragging the excellent down to their own level, for the accusation of being elitist (of being the best, really), evokes the fear of being called undemocratic. With characteristic cunning Screwtape tells his audience: "What I want to fix your attention on is the vast, overall movement toward the discrediting, and finally the elimination, of every kind of human excellence — moral, cultural, social, or intellectual."[22]

It is not without significance, perhaps, that many world mythologies contain stories of some kind of precosmic degeneration, some kind of fall, from the very exalted realm of the divine, or spirit, or light, to the ordinary, frivolous realm of darkness. Adam and Eve are cast out, Sophia falls, the Soul turns toward matter, the Light is captured by darkness.[23] A Mandaean source has Spirit bewail her exile: "My eyes, which were opened from the abode of light, now belong to the [body-] stump. My heart, which longs for the Life, came here and was made part of the stump."[24] It is as if we, dwellers of Middle Earth (Midgard, in the Norse myth), envious of the superlative beauty and wisdom of the gods (the Aesir, in the Norse myth, dwelling in Asgard), had to drag them down to our own level and deprive them of all their excellence, drawing comfort in the fact that now we are all equally destitute and equally prosaic.

An example of this is the fate of schooling in America. When the decision was made in the 1840s to broaden the schooling opportunities for all, education had to be narrowed, for the majority were incapable of understanding the classical education then being dispensed in private academies and seminaries. Misled by a misapplication of the notion of democracy, the reformers decided that if schooling was going to be available to all, then the content had to be made accessible to all as well, a goal that required the lowering of standards. Where education had hearkened to the call to excellence along the lines of Peleus's advice to his son, the goal became to succeed at the tasks set before the students. Where truth used to manifest itself to a few in flashes of insight, it became what any fool can see. In the words of Norman O. Brown:

> The pristine academies were esoteric and aristocratic, self-consciously separate from the profane vulgar. Democratic resentment denies that there can be anything that can't be seen by everybody; in the democratic academy truth is subject to public verification; truth is what any fool can see. This is what is meant by the so-called scientific method: so-called science is the attempt to democratize knowledge — the attempt to substitute method for insight, mediocrity for genius, by getting a standardized operating procedure. The great equalizers dispensed by the scientific method are the tools, those analytical tools. The miracle of genius is replaced by the standardized mechanism. But fools with tools are still fools.[25]

Except that in a frivolous culture few seem to notice and fewer still seem to care.

ON DIVERSION

Van Ness defines diversion as keeping the mind active in matters of inconsequence.[26] This is commonly the case in our culture, where diversion seems to be the order of the day. Most entertainment is ultimately unimportant and unsatisfying because there is no point to it, no point of ultimate concern. So why would we produce and engage in such frivolous matters? Pascal suggests that the reason is "the natural poverty of our feeble and mortal condition, so miserable that nothing can comfort us when we think of it closely."[27] If this rather gloomy view were true, it would mean, among other things, that the various forms of entertainment, from gambling to drinking to tennis to football, all have at their root an inner need for diversion, for distraction, born from the emptiness surrounding our lives. Diversion, then, can be seen as an effort to shift our mental gaze from the contemplation of our state on earth to something less significant, less important but more pleasing — at least in the short term — and less stressful.

One danger is that one may get used to doing this and to the resulting easy life without depth, the life of hollow people about whom so much has been written in modern times, a life that pervades so much of our experience today that we no longer seem to notice it. Writing about the Quakers in eighteenth century America, John Woolman, himself a Quaker, expressed concern about the fact that his coreligionists had become accustomed to luxuries which were not at all necessary for a good life.   But what concerned him the most about the traffic in "superfluities," as he called them, was the fact that "dimness of sight came over many," with the consequent "neglect [of] the pure feeling of truth."[28]

I should not like to give the impression that all diversions are bad, though some undoubtedly are, at least to some of those involved in them. Montaigne cites the case of Atalanta, an invincible Amazonian runner who had decided not to marry except to the man who could defeat her. Eventually she lost control of her life when, in a race set up for her suitors, she was distracted thrice by the golden apples thrown her way by the suitor Hippomenes, whom she would have soundly defeated otherwise. Going after the golden orbs she lost the race and, with the loss, her virginity, though it must be added that she was deliberately forced off course by a somewhat jealous Aphrodite.[29]

We read a similar story about Tio Conejo (called Brer Rabbit in American folklore), who was able to divert the attention of Señor Tigre and thus escaped unharmed. It seems that Tio Conejo was making a rope one day when he was surprised by Señor Tigre in such a way that he could not escape. Realizing that his end was near, Tio Conejo said, "OK, eat me right now. I don't want to be around when — it happens."

"What is going to happen?"

"Oh, you haven't heard? A terrible hurricane is coming this way; it will be here soon. I was fashioning a rope to tie myself to a tree and save myself."

"Good idea," said Señor Tigre. "Would you tie me down, too?"

"Sure," said Tio Conejo, as he proceeded to tie Señor Tigre to a tree and forthwith made his escape.[30] Here, too, the diversion was not good for Señor Tigre, who was duped by it, but it certainly saved the life of Brer Rabbit.

It was good, too, for Shahrazad, the Wezir's daughter who offered herself as sexual partner to King Shahriyar even with the knowledge that she would be put to death the next morning. As she was introduced to the King,

> she wept, so he said to her, "What aileth thee?" She answered, "O King, I have a young sister, and I wish to take leave of her." So the King sent for her; and she came to her sister, and embraced her, and sat near the foot of the bed; and after she had waited for a proper opportunity, she said, "By Allah! O my sister. Relate to us a story to beguile the waking hour of our night." "Most willingly," answered Shahrazad, if this virtuous King permit me." And the King, hearing these words, and being restless, was pleased with the idea of listening to the story; and thus, on the first night of the thousand and one, Shahrazad commenced her recitations.[31]

It would appear that after a diversion lasting nearly three years, the King must have understood and Shahrazad would have been assured of her life. In her case, the clever stratagem had worked for her good.

Most diversions, then, have a certain ambiguity to them, favoring some and proving harmful to others. There are some, however, that have no redeeming value whatsoever, for they imperil the soul and always lead to ruin. The problem is to discern which diversions might be harmful and which might not. The Gospels ask the question in general, "What good is it to win the whole world if the soul is lost?"[32] but no specifics are given. Faust accepted the bargain and managed to beat Mephistopheles in the end, though he had help from Gretchen. One thing is sure: where diversions are frivolous and inconsequential, we might do well to be forewarned.

CONCLUSION

Confucius already commented that frivolous people will lose the respect of their peers.[33] Who wants to snorkel when you can be a deep sea diver? Some are frivolous because they do not know anything better, just as many grow up with biases they often tend not to know they have. In religion, especially, there is a world of deep scholarship that remains locked away and unavailable to the superficial believer, partly because religious leaders find it easier to control the ignorant, partly because the trivial is always easier to stomach, takes less effort and is not likely to upset anybody. Everybody knows what a hamburger is, but ostrich steak? Or Chilean sea bass? Or Spanish morcilla? People flock to buy "schlock" art; but a Mondrian? Supermarkets sell cheap novels written according to a formula; but the works of Schiller? Or of George Sand? I wonder how many CDs has Hildegard von Bingen sold, though the magic of her music is still alive after a thousand years.

Trying to alter the frivolous presents a daunting task, for one must first convince people that what they relish is rubbish and that they should give it up. I have witnessed this phenomenon often in college freshmen. They strut into their universities with behaviors and ideas that made them stand out in high school, but now they are told such things are superficial, trivial, frivolous, and that they must transcend them and grow up. And eventually most do. But how do you do this to a forty-year-old person? How does one help people realize that what they think is good is rubbish, that what they deem deep is shallow, that what they treat as serious is frivolous? And yet, as Marcuse wrote, "all liberation depends on the consciousness of servitude";[34] that is, there is no way to freedom unless one knows one is enslaved. But the problem arises when the fetters are things one has won, when the fetters are disguised as silky bows, when they are made to seem good. There is no higher obstacle to a better life than a good life, especially when this life is better than one's parents' life. How to break through this psychological barrier? Plato's Socrates suggested facetiously that the way to reform could begin only with the exile of everybody above ten years of age, an obvious impossibility,[35] and during the 1960s the recommendation was not to trust anyone over thirty. How does one wean people away from their "soaps"? Yet if the connection of humor with faith is to flourish, humor must rise to the heights of faith. In order to do this it must cease to be frivolous.

NOTES

1. Elaine Kendall, *The Happy Mediocrity* (New York: G. P. Putnam's Sons, 1971), p. 112.

On Frivolity   101

2. Leo Tolstoy, *War and Peace*, Book VI, Chapter 18, in *Great Books of the Western World*, Robert M. Hutchins, ed. (Chicago: Encyclopaedia Britannica, 1952), Vol. 51, p. 261.

3. José Ortega y Gasset, *The Revolt of the Masses* (New York: W. W. Norton & Co., Inc., 1957), p. 108.

4. Ibid., p. 13.

5. Ibid., p. 18.

6. José Ortega y Gasset, *Mission of the University* (New York: W. W. Norton & Co., Inc., 1966), pp. 38-39.

7. Ortega, *The Revolt of the Masses*, p. 112.

8. Friedrich Nietzsche, *Schopenhauer as Educator*, James W. Hillesheim and Malcolm R. Simpson, transl. (Chicago: Henry Regnery Co., 1965), Chapter 1.

9. Ibid., p. 3.

10. Ray Bradbury, *Fahrenheit 451* (New York: Ballantine Books, 1991), p. 20.

11. Paraphrasing Nietzsche, *Schopenhauer as Educator*, p. 5.

12. Hermann Hesse, *The Glass Bead Game* (New York: Henry Holt & Co., Inc., 1990), pp. 19-20.

13. Ibid., p. 18.

14. Carl E. Schorske, *Fin-de-Siècle Vienna: Politics and Culture* (New York: Alfred A. Knopf, 1980), pp. 9-10.

15. Benjamin Anastas, *An Underachiever's Diary* (New York: The Dial Press, 1998).

16. Ibid., p. 116.

17. Ibid., pp. 146-147.

18. *The Iliad* XI, 784, in *Great Books of the Western World*, Robert M. Hutchins, ed. (Chicago: Encyclopedia Britannica, 1952).

19. Anastas, *Underachiever's Diary*, p. 145.

20. Hesse, *Steppenwolf* (New York: Holt, Rinehart & Winston, 1963), p. 155.

21. C. S. Lewis, *The Screwtape Letters* (New York: Macmillan, 1962), pp. 161-163.

22. Ibid., pp. 164-165.

23. Hans Jonas, *Gnosticism* (Boston: Beacon Press, 1963), pp. 62-65.

24. *Ginza: Der Schatz oder das Grosse Buch der Mandäer*, M. Lidzbarski, transl. (Göttingen, 1925), p. 454, quoted in Jonas, *Gnosticism*, p. 67.

25. Norman O. Brown, "Apocalypse: The Place of Mystery in the Life of the Mind," in *The Movement toward a New America*, Mitchell Goodman, ed. (New York: Alfred Knopf, 1970), p. 629.

26. Peter H. Van Ness, *Spirituality, Diversion, and Decadence* (Albany: State University of New York Press, 1992), p. 78.

27. Blaise Pascal, *Pensées*, #139 (New York: E. P. Dutton & Co., 1958).

28. John Woolman, *The Journal of John Woolman*, Chapter XII, in *The Harvard Classics*, Charles W. Eliot, ed. (New York: P. F. Collier and Son Corp., 1965), p. 305.

29. Ovid, *Metamorphoses* X. 677, Rolfe Humphries, transl. (Bloomington: Indiana University Press, 1964), p. 256. Michel Eyquem de Montaigne, *The Essays*, III. 4, in *Great Books of the Western World*, Robert M. Hutchins, ed. (Chicago: Encyclopedia Britannica, 1952), Vol. 25, p. 402.

30. Mary Ann Brewer, "Tío Conejo and the Hurricane," in *Treasury of North American Folk Tales*, Catherine Peck, ed. (New York: Quality Paperback Book Club, 1998), pp. 210-212.

31. *Stories from The Thousand and One Nights*, Edward William Lane, transl. *The Harvard Classics*, Charles W. Eliot, ed. (New York: P. F. Collier & Son Corp., 1965), Vol. 16, p. 13.

32. *Matthew* 16:26.

33. Confucius, *The Analects*, Arthur Waley, transl. (New York: Vintage, 1938), Book I, 8, p. 85.

34. Herbert Marcuse, *One-Dimensional Man* (Boston: Beacon Press, 1964), p. 7.

35. Plato, *Republic* VII. 540.

8

Humor and Faith

Throughout his life and his major works, Kierkegaard sought to elucidate what he thought were the three major stages of a serious person's life. Books such as *Either/Or* (1843), *Fear and Trembling* (1843), *Stages on Life's Way* (1845), and *Concluding Unscientific Postscript* (1846), analyze in considerable, even prolix detail what he meant by these stages, the aesthetic, the ethical, and the religious. In his own words, "while aesthetic existence is essentially enjoyment, and ethical existence, essentially struggle and victory, religious existence is essentially suffering."[1] Explaining Kierkegaard's statement, Louis Mackey writes:

> An aesthete's life is organized around pleasure, an ethical life around the opposition between good and evil. The religious life is a life in which *God* is acknowledged as the sole sufficient point of reference for human existence. Reflection on the nature of God shows that such a life is necessarily a life of suffering.[2]

I would not say that the religious life is necessarily one of suffering, though it certainly is one of struggle, for the daily confrontation with the absurd is no walk in the park; but then, again, there is humor to relieve this struggle. Even Sisyphus, who, Camus said, must be deemed happy in his struggle with his rock, must have smiled every time he remembered the trick he had played on the gods!

The aesthetic life — meaning the experiential and sensual life, according to the original, Greek meaning of the term $\alpha\check{\iota}\sigma\theta\eta\sigma\iota\varsigma$, sensory perception — is a direct or immediate life.[3] It is the life in which one is what one is in the perceivable world, where one's actions have objective consequences and one's life is lived at the external, physical, or material level, as it were, so that it can be easily apprehended and described.[4] It would not be altogether false to say it is superficial, and this is its weakness.

The second sphere is that of the ethical, the sphere of ambiguities and dualities, the sphere of requirements and obligations, where one becomes what one becomes. In it one moves oneself from the aesthetic and external in an effort of internality.

According to Kierkegaard, the ethical is not a dwelling place but only a passageway to be crossed again and again in one's life.

The third sphere is the religious one, the time of fulfillment, where one stands alone before God always considering oneself in transit. Here the internal life develops to the fullest, and the externality of the aesthetic is viewed as a test or trial of one's faith.[5]   Kierkegaard distinguished between two levels of religiosity, Religiousness A and Religiousness B or, simply, Christianity.

Religiousness A is essentially immanent. In it one discovers one's limits vis-à-vis the transcendent, but the emphasis is on oneself, on one's limitations and shortcomings. In Religiousness B one moves toward the transcendent and para-doxical, therefore it is the realm of faith, of the willingness to open oneself up to the obscurity of the beyond. For this is what faith is, "the ideality that resolves an *esse* in a *non posse* and now *wills* to believe it";[6] that is, the conception that uncovers an impossibility in what is and then holds on to it willfully through an act of faith.

> *The Religiousness A* comprehends the contradiction as suffering in self-annihilation, although within immanence, but by ethically accentuating the fact of existing it prevents the exister from becoming abstract in immanence, or from becoming abstract by wishing to remain in immanence. *The paradoxical religiousness* [Religiousness B] breaks with immanence and makes the fact of existing the absolute contradiction, not within immanence, but against immanence. There is no longer any immanent fundamental kinship between the temporal and the eternal, because the eternal itself has entered time and would constitute there the kinship.[7]

Kierkegaard thinks that Religiousness B marks Christianity as well as any other view that makes faith an encounter with paradox, as do Buddhism, Judaism, and Islam[8] — that is, any view in which the believer can be drawn into the paradoxical like an item into the funnel of a tornado.

It follows that Kierkegaard sees humor as the essential condition for the religious life — not so much for Religiousness A as for Religiousness B, the stage where the individual confronts the Unknown as wholly transcendent and incomprehensible. Those who cannot see humor as quintessentially religious live merely at the level of Religiousness A or below. Put differently, those who cannot laugh cannot be Christians — or Jews, or Muslims, or Buddhists. Kierkegaard writes: "The question of the legitimacy of the comic, of its relationship to the religious, of whether it does not have a place in the religious address itself — this question is of essential significance for a religious existence in our times."[9]

Much of the meaning of Kierkegaard's statement is implicit in the materials already presented. In order to demonstrate more explicitly the religious significance of humor, it must be shown how humor, because of its structure, preserves the paradoxical truth of faith, how it leads to mystery, the mystery of "the divine incognito," and why, therefore, it must be learned.

TRUTH PRESERVED: SOCRATES AND MARK TWAIN

Socrates has come down to us as the great master ironist. Whether the picture is accurate or only a Platonic fiction, the fact is that no other figure in history, with the exception of Jesus, has exerted such an attraction despite the ambiguity endemic in all ironic statements. Commenting on the irony of Socrates as portrayed in the Platonic dialogues, Friedländer writes: "As in a Greek statue the garment not only serves as a veil but at the same time reveals that which it veils, so is Plato's irony also a guide on the path to the eternal forms and to that which is beyond being."[10] It is part of Plato's art — and it was part of Socrates's method — to pursue his inquiries not always directly but through the means of irony, denying when he meant to affirm, and affirming when he intended to deny, always in an atmosphere suffused with humor and prankish playfulness. If anyone ever deserved the title "the laughing philosopher" it was not Democritus[11] but Plato's Socrates.

Irony, of course, is different from humor, though perhaps the connection between them is very intimate. Kierkegaard, among others, studied irony at length, especially with reference to Socrates;[12] he came to the conclusion that humor is more fundamental than irony — even a transcendental category.[13] The point here is not to restate his arguments but to take a cue from him, and to indicate how at the time when Greek philosophical speculation begins in real earnest, it is not under the aegis of seriousness but of playful humor that it takes off. It should be a matter of profound consequence, something to wonder at, that Socrates, at the beginning of the Western intellectual tradition, did not disdain to pursue the most serious questions humans can ask through the means of playful banter. If, as Whitehead once remarked, all Western philosophy is but a footnote to Plato, one must wonder why the footnote is so pompous when the main text is so light and airy. Against this background it is easy to understand how Erasmus could poke fun at the philosophers and theologians of his day; he saw them so lost in serious speculation as to appear foolish and derisible.[14] On the other hand, and in another time, the profundity of the subject did not deter Socrates from conducting his inquiry in a playful manner.

The main point to be noted here is that the truth in question, whatever it be, however taxing and challenging, however paradoxical in nature, is not betrayed, diminished, or obliterated because of humor. Freud saw a truth behind every joke and witticism. In a more profound sense, humor is the preserver of truth. It should therefore not seem surprising that where the perception of truth has been most profound it has also been presented humorously — that is, paradoxically: Socrates, Diogenes, Buddha, Jesus, Lao-tzu, Chuang-tzu. That many of their followers failed to laugh and have remained, in some cases, overwrought with seriousness for millennia is due to their own lack of a sense of humor, not to the original orientation of the masters. "What forbids laughing while we tell the truth?" asked Horace.[15] What, indeed? "Suppose the world were only one of God's jokes," G. B. Shaw wrote to Tolstoy in 1910, "would you work any the less to make it a good joke instead of a bad one?"[16] Where is the truth diminished because we couch it in the humor of a joke? The reason for this has been stated above: both the tragic and the comic are apprehensions, ways of seizing phenomena. Facts are facts; what allows us to laugh or cry in their presence is our perception of them as tragic or comic. In either case, the facts remain what they are.

Take the work of Mark Twain. It is steeped, as Brodwin has pointed out, in a humor that "ultimately derives from contradiction, absurdity and incongruity, the principle of irony triumphant."[17] The reason is obvious: humor does not detract from the veracity of any statement. Arising as it does out of contradiction, it always maintains the ambiguity that gave it birth. The paradox of faith is preserved in the paradox of humor, the contradiction of faith in the contradiction of the joke. Humor, therefore, is no betrayer of the truth; on the contrary, it is its preserver. Take the story of the temptation of Adam and Eve and their Fall from Paradise: it is a serious story if you read the *Genesis* account and the thousand sermons and commentaries on it with a serious intent; it is, however, a comic story as retold by Mark Twain: "Adam," he concludes, "was but human — this explains it all. He did not want the apple for the apple's sake, he wanted it because it was forbidden. The mistake was in not forbidding the serpent; then he would have eaten the serpent."[18] Twain's story is the same as that in the *Genesis* account, even though his retelling of it is amusing. The moral of the story is not less true because it is hilarious. The same can be said of Trudeau's retelling of Solomon's "Judgment story" in *Doonesbury*, or of Schulz's theological comments in *Peanuts*.[19] It must be clear, therefore, that humor, however lighthearted it be, does not betray the truth of faith or the irreconcilable nature of paradox. In fact, humor preserves paradox, since it is born out of it and leads its existence in total dependence on it.

THE IMPERATIVE OF LAUGHTER: NIETZSCHE AND HESSE

It is impossible to encapsulate in a few paragraphs everything Nietzsche wrote about humor. His thoughts on humor are ultimately tied to his ideas on play and dance, and they all form part of what he understood to be the fundamental and vital spirit of the earth, the Dionysian. Nothing has value apart from the Dionysian. Indeed, it is from the Dionysian that everything that is truly human inevitably proceeds.

"I estimate the value of men, of races," Nietzsche writes, "according to the necessity by which they cannot conceive the god apart from the satyr."[20] For the Greeks, the satyr was a woodsy minor god, follower of Dionysus and generally the incarnation of lustful appetites. Though human in form, he had the hoofed legs, beard, and horns of a goat. The true god is thus Dionysus, the inspirer of revelers, the model of the satyr, in whose honor first in the villages, and later on in the cities, were enacted the mysteries of life amidst the sounds of music and the movements of dance. Nietzsche himself could only have believed in a god who could dance.[21]

Nietzsche interprets the so-called Sermon on the Mount (it is really a loosely organized collection of sayings), especially the Beatitudes, as a denial of laughter. If there is denial in the pronouncements of Jesus it is only by implication: laughter is not specifically mentioned, much less damned, but seriousness and the enduring of sorrow are indeed extolled, and rejoicing is promised only at a future date, in an afterlife — which by itself should be taken as a commendation of laughter. The praise of seriousness, says Nietzsche, has led to a downgrading of laughter. Indeed, according to him, laughter has become the great sin: "'Woe unto those who laugh here!'"[22] he interprets Jesus as saying — rather, as implying. Needless to say, two thousand years of Christianity have consistently emphasized the value of sorrow and of seriousness and the frivolity of laughter.

Against this tradition Nietzsche preaches the importance of humor, the holiness of laughter. "Nothing succeeds if prankishness has no part in it,"[23] he writes. Zarathustra crowns himself with holy laughter,[24] and in his exhortation to the "higher men," he bursts forth with the categorical imperative: "You higher men, *learn* to laugh!"[25] — that is, you who strive to be the best human beings, learn to laugh! This is a most welcome recommendation, but it is still permissible to ask, *Why* is laughter *holy? Why* must one not merely laugh but especially *learn* to laugh?

The world and life provide us with innumerable opportunities for laughter because they offer countless experiences of paradox and contradiction. Contradiction is the soil in which humor's roots are sunk. As long as this soil remains, the roots cannot lack nourishment. There are thus plenty of reasons to laugh.

Contradictions abound because they are the inevitable result of human inquiry. We want to understand, we want everything to be explained to us, and in our relentless drive towards comprehensiveness we push our systems to their very limits. The systems eventually recoil upon themselves, bite their own tails like the uroboros — and suddenly a new breakthrough is achieved.[26] The coiling of systems upon themselves, important though it is, can generate diverse reactions. The demise of the Ptolemaic system and the emergence of the Copernican are matters of profound indifference with respect to the meaning of life. On the other hand, the very question of the meaning of life often drives men and women to their deaths.[27] This confrontation with the absurd and with the paradoxical in our lives, this coming of mind to the end of its tether renders us shaken, bewildered, nauseated, incapable of action. In matters that concern us intimately, no exit means we are trapped, unable to move.

When such a situation arises, says Nietzsche, we need to move beyond the system: we need an illusion, a game, by means of which we may move beyond frustration. Etymologically, illusion (from Latin *in–*, into, and *lusus*, game) means entering into a game. Humor provides the alibi. It is a game. The comic, according to Nietzsche, is precisely "the artistic discharge of the nausea of absurdity."[28] Laughter momentarily diffuses and disarms paradox.

Laughter is holy because it is salvific. It is salvation from the clutches of the absurd. Not that the absurd is dissolved, but that it loses its sting, its power to withhold action, its power to negate enterprise. It is through laughter that one denies contradiction its power to prevent progress, to impede transcendence. Laughter propels beyond the system coiled upon itself.

Nietzsche expresses the holy character of laughter by associating seriousness with the devil. "The devil is the spirit of gravity," he says;[29] the devil is "serious, thorough, profound, and solemn . . . through him all things fall!"[30] The devil would tie us to seriousness so that remaining fixed in the paradox we may not do anything — least of all move beyond. Against such evil, laughter is the best exorcism: "Come, let us kill the spirit of gravity!"[31] — that is, let us laugh!

The categorical imperative follows from all this: one must learn to laugh.

Nietzsche does not mean to say that any silly laughter is enough to achieve the passage beyond paradox to the mystery. Silly laughter need not be learned; it comes to us spontaneously. This is the nonhumorous laughter described above, the result of tickling, or of sheer good feeling, or the innocent laughter of children. No; the laughter that Nietzsche would have us learn is the laughter that arises vis-à-vis the absurd, the cracking of a joke in sight of chaos or in the radius of the collapsing Twin Towers.

There is another way to express this. In its absoluteness and infinity, truth is incomprehensible. It is *mystery*. It discloses itself partially here and there, in this system and in that, but it cannot be comprehended by any system. Even to state the truth is to betray it, insofar as it is to encapsulate it in a system of words. It is important, therefore, to realize not merely that Truth is incomprehensible, but that the very formulation of this incomprehensibility betrays it. Only those who have forgotten that Truth is incomprehensible try to understand this incom-prehensibility and to state it in the words of a system. Conversely, what can be formulated and stated about the incomprehensibility of Truth bears little resemblance to the mystery. Conclusion: in the presence of mystery the proper response is silence — or laughter.[32]

Hermann Hesse deals with this topic in his delightful and profound novel, *The Journey to the East*.[33] H. H., who is a "defector" from the League of Journeyers to the East, is trying to write the story of the League and its Journey, but finds himself frustrated in his endeavors. He cannot remember any details or important data — essentially, as he discovers later, because to wish to write the unwritable story of the League is possible only for someone who has already forgotten what the League is. Conversely, whatever can be written by such a person bears little, if any, resemblance to what the League really is.

Such paradox begets laughter. This is what Hesse means by stating that all humor is gallows-humor.[34] He adds: "To live in the world as if it were not the world, to observe the law and yet to be above it, to possess 'as though one did not possess,' to renounce as though no renunciation were involved — only humor is able to live up to these revered and often formulated demands of a noble philosophy of life."[35] It is the Immortals, the great human beings — the Buddhas, Goethes, Mozarts — who have achieved this profound insight. Harry Haller, who aspires to become one of them, is therefore directed to learn to laugh, eventually entering the Magic Theater, that marvelous "school of humor."[36] No tuition is demanded in this school; only that the student cease to take himself seriously and laugh heartily at himself, that is, at that absurd and paradoxical mixture that every self is, composed as it is of a myriad opposite, warring selves.

Harry Haller did not learn his lesson in school. Marvelous though the institution was, and wonderful and famous though the teachers were, he was unable, when the final test came, to put aside his seriousness and laugh at the paradoxes of life. Mozart had advised him, "All life is so, my child, and we must let it be so; and if we are not asses laugh at it. . . . Learn what is to be taken seriously and laugh at the rest."[37] But Harry Haller would not accept this simple lesson. Therefore he was found guilty of showing himself devoid of humor and was dismissed from the school, hounded out by "one simultaneous peal of laughter, a laughter in full chorus, a frightful laughter of the other world that is scarcely to be borne by the ears of men."[38]

Haller was surprised. He had thought he would have to forfeit his life. In fact, he mused, better to die than to live confronted by paradox. But the sentence condemned him "to live and to learn to laugh,"[39] to live in the presence of the absurd and to learn the magic attitude toward mystery — laughter, the humor attitude.

HUMOR AND TERROR

At a crucial juncture in Golding's novel, *Lord of the Flies*, young Simon stands resolute before the Lord of the Flies, sticking to his discovery that the feared Beast is nothing but a pig's head on a stick. Then comes the second insight: "Fancy thinking that the beast was something you could hunt and kill!" And for a moment or two the entire forest echoed with the parody of laughter,[40] a laughter similar to the one that accompanied Don Giovanni on his way to hell.

At a parallel place in Hesse's *Steppenwolf*, Harry Haller hears "behind him a peal of laughter, a clear and ice-cold laughter out of a world unknown to men . . . born of divine humor."[41] Mozart instructs him that he must put off his seriousness and learn to laugh, reminding him that "humor is always gallows-humor,"[42] and that therefore it must be tested against the reality of terror and death. It is not without reason that in America, the greatest comedians and humorists have been Jews, African-Americans, and, lately, women — that is, people who, due to the vicissitudes of history, have had to look at terror and injustice in the face, and laugh. It is this characteristic of humor that, more than others, distinguishes it from mere fun and vain jocularity.

When Abraham climbed Mount Moriah to sacrifice his only son, Isaac, the Lord stayed his hand and, in Woody Allen's account, said to him, "How could thou doest such a thing?"

> And Abraham said, "But thou said — "
> "Never mind what I said," the Lord spake. "Doth thou listen to every crazy idea that comes thy way?" And Abraham grew ashamed. "Er — not really . . . no."
> "I jokingly suggest thou sacrifice Isaac and thou immediately runs out to do it."
> And Abraham fell to his knees, "See, I never know when you're kidding."
> And the Lord thundered, "No sense of humor, I can't believe it."[43]

The association of humor and terror should not seem surprising. Edmund Burke related terror to fear and both to the sublime, noting that in many languages the same word signifies both terror and astonishment or admiration.[44] Rudolf Otto describes the *tremendum*, a category of the holy, as an overwhelming fear that is more than fear proper and that the Greeks named ὀργή θεοῦ ("wrath of god") or δεῖμα Πανικόν ("the horror of Pan"), and Denis de Rougemont experienced as "sacred horror" when he stood in the midst of a crowd gone crazy in its adulation of the Führer.[45]

Writing about his experiences in a Nazi concentration camp, Viktor Frankl took pains to show how humor was present in the camp. It may have been momentary and at times subdued, but the prisoners were able to find a sense of humor even in the midst of the desolation of the camp and the omnipresence of suffering.[46]

The point is that humor, rather than being overshadowed by terror, can confront it as few other human attitudes can. Legend has it that Sir Thomas More, as his head was being placed on the executioner's block, requested that his beard be spared because, he quipped, "it had done no wrong"![47]

THE TRANSPARENCY OF LAUGHTER

We have seen that for Kierkegaard the comic arises out of contradiction and paradox. But Kierkegaard showed also that contradiction does not necessitate the comic reaction. The comic reaction is possible only if one has developed the humorous attitude, if one has learned to laugh.

Kierkegaard contrasted the comic reaction with the tragic. For him, there are two fundamental attitudes to paradox, the tragic or pathetic and the comic. The tragic attitude confronts paradox in terms of systems, of logic, and of reasons, and insofar as it confronts paradox this way, the tragic attitude binds itself to the insolubility of the paradox in a hopeless manner: it despairs of a way out and therefore experiences suffering, anguish, frustration. The comic attitude, on the other hand, looks at paradox in terms of mystery. It envisages the beyond where paradox is the mystery of the coincidence of opposites, and therefore it experiences no pain.[48] Kierkegaard writes: "The law for the comical is quite simple: it exists wherever there is a contradiction, and where the contradiction is painless because it is viewed as canceled; for the comical does not indeed cancel the contradiction, but a legitimate comical apprehension can do so [momentarily], otherwise it is not legitimate."[49] As Kierkegaard would put it metaphorically, the tragic apprehension gazes at paradox in the light of systems, while the comic gazes at paradox in the light of mystery.[50] It is all a matter of where the light comes from that illumines the paradox. Thus it is narrated that Epictetus, the slave boy of Epaphroditus — a fat and ample man, by all accounts — was once punished by the master who sat on his leg while berating him. "You are going to break it," warned Epictetus. The pressure increased and the leg broke with a loud crack, at which point Epictetus quipped calmly, "I told you!"[51]

There is a further implication here, however. Not every light reaches the object to be illuminated. The most powerful source of light can be blocked by diverse opaque substances. The result is an eclipse and a consequent darkness upon the object. Kierkegaard's suggestion that humor seek to see paradox illumined by the Divine Light carries with it the implication that humor is transparent. It does not eclipse the mystery. It constitutes itself into a vehicle of light precisely because, by its very nature, it is "a way out," an opening. Thus it is the attitude *par excellence* with which to approach the paradoxes that specifically confront the individual who is ultimately and intimately concerned. Indeed, as Kierkegaard shows, those who are passionately interested in their own salvation, or in the ultimate meaning of their lives, cannot find the answer in the objective, logical theories offered them by philosophers and theologians. A subjective thirst cannot be quenched by objective facts.[52] Confronting such objectivity engenders only the tragic attitude and despair of a way out. Only a subjective appropriation such as is possible in jest or play — and in faith — enables individuals to orient themselves towards the infinite, towards what alone can assuage their thirst without ever stilling it altogether. For, after all, even in faith the paradox is not explained away.

CONCLUSION

From this point of view humor is *propisteutic* ("faith engendering"). It enables the individual to transcend the paradox momentarily in a joke. But in doing so it points necessarily to the beyond wherein the paradox is incorporated into the infinite coincidence of all opposites. Humor opens the doors momentarily to mystery; faith alone can make the opening permanent. Humor is a transparent inkling into mystery; to hold oneself permanently in mystery is faith.

It should be pointed out that while different, there is no fundamental opposition between the tragic and the comic. They supplement each other. The tragic sense entails the deliberate effort never to dissolve the paradox, never to water down the tenets of faith, never to let go the horns of the dilemma. Given this effort, tragedy reigns, and no laughter is possible. The comic sense, on the other hand, makes believe there is a way out through a joke — although it knows all the time there is none. And it also knows that such knowing is unutterable. It pretends there is an utterance, knowing all the time that there is none. Tragic faith sees God become man and keeps silence. Comic faith sees God slip on a banana peel and tumble into a mess of flesh — and it laughs.

Now, it is a fact that most contemporary faith is stained by a tragic tint. Our faith is humorless. There are far too many among us who can see only the tragic aspect of life. Moreover, many argue that in the aftermath of two World Wars, the Holocaust, the Killing Fields, and the World Trade Center, one would betray reality if one laughed. But this position misses the point. Laughter that is born of humor does not deny the paradoxes of war, of crime, of injustice, and of our inhumanity to our own kind. Humor merely laughs because it pretends, in the flashing exhilaration of the joke, that there is a way out — the way of faith.

The comic spirit is greatly needed today. It is needed because there is so much cause to believe in a tragic sense; because so many people take themselves and the world in which they live too seriously; because too many people are incapable of laughing while believing. We need to inject quite a bit of humor into our faith. We need to believe with a clownish spirit. What better way is there to believe the paradoxes of faith?

Moreover, *we* need to learn to believe and laugh. For if we do not do it, then laughter, humor, the comic, are overcome by the trite, the merely "funny," the trivial, and the infantile kind of laughter that generally pervades what is called today "entertainment." We should not let humor be restricted to the silly, the superficial, the idiotic. We should learn to believe with humor so that our humor itself may be solidly based. Faith that excludes the comic is dangerously morbid and grudging; faith that excludes the tragic is immature; but the fullness of faith calls forth both joy and maturity — that is, both humor and steadfast effort to maintain the truth that is the paradox.

NOTES

1. Søren Kierkegaard, *Concluding Unscientific Postscript* (Princeton, NJ: Princeton University Press, 1968), p. 256.

2. Louis Mackey, "Søren Kierkegaard: The Poetry of Inwardness," in *Existential Philosophers: Kierkegaard to Merleau-Ponty*, George Alfred Schrader, Jr., ed. (New York: McGraw-Hill Book Co., 1967), p. 75.

3. Søren Kierkegaard, *Stages on Life's Way* (Princeton: Princeton University Press, 1988), p. 476.

4. Ibid., p. 441.

5. Ibid., pp. 442-443.

6. Ibid., p. 440.

7. Kierkegaard, *Concluding Unscientific Postscript*, pp. 507-508.

8. Ibid., p. 512.

9. Kierkegaard, p. 459.

10. Paul Friedländer, *Plato* (New York: Pantheon Books, 1958), Vol. I, p. 153.

11. Erasmus, *Praise of Folly* (London: Penguin Books, 1971), p. 49.

12. Søren Kierkegaard, *The Concept of Irony* (Bloomington, IN: Indiana University Press, 1968).

13. Ibid., p. 341.

14. Erasmus, *Praise of Folly*, pp. 52-53.

15. Horace, *The Satires*, Lib. I, 1, in *The Satires, Epistles and the Ars Poetica*, H. Rushton Fairclough, transl. *The Loeb Classical Library*. Cambridge, MA: Harvard University Press, 1926.

16. George B. Shaw, *Collected Letters*, 1898-1910, Dan H. Laurence, ed. (New York: Viking, 1985), p. 902.

17. Stanley Brodwin, "The Humor of the Absurd: Mark Twain's Adamic Diaries," *Criticism* 14:1 (Winter, 1972), p. 49.

18. Mark Twain, *Pudd'nhead Wilson*, in *The Family Mark Twain* (New York: Harper & Row, 1972), Ch. 2.

19. Robert L. Short, *The Gospel According to Peanuts* (Richmond, VA: John Knox Press, 1965). Also Karl-Josef Kuschel, *Laughter: A Theological Reflection* (New York: 1994.

20. Friedrich Nietzsche, *Ecce Homo* (New York: Vintage, 1967), "Why I am so clever," p. 4.

21. Friedrich Nietzsche, *Thus Spoke Zarathustra* (New York: Viking, 1966), I, 7.

22. Ibid., IV, 13, 16.

23. Friedrich Nietzsche, *Twilight of the Idols* (New York: Vintage, 1968), p. 465.

24. Nietzsche, *Thus Spoke Zarathustra*, IV, 13, 18.

25. Ibid., IV, 13, 20.

26. Friedrich Nietzsche, *The Birth of Tragedy* (New York: Vintage, 1967), Section 15, pp. 97-98.

27. Albert Camus, *The Myth of Sisyphus* (New York: Vintage, 1955), pp. 3-4.

28. Nietzsche, *The Birth of Tragedy*, Section 7, p. 60.

29. Nietzsche, *Zarathustra*, II, 10, p. 107.

30. Ibid., I, 7, p. 41.

31. Ibid.

32. Karl Jaspers, *Nietzsche* (Chicago: Gateway Editions, 1969), p. 220.

33. Hermann Hesse, *The Journey to the East*, Hilda Rosner, transl. (London: P. Owen, 1964).

34. Hermann Hesse, *Steppenwolf* (New York: Holt, Rinehart & Winston, 1963), p. 214.

35. Ibid., p. 55.

36. Ibid., p. 177.

37. Ibid., p. 213.

38. Ibid., p. 215.

39. Ibid., p. 216.

40. William Golding, *Lord of the Flies* (New York: Capricorn Books, 1959), pp. 132-133.

41. Hesse, *Steppenwolf*, p. 204.

42. Ibid., p. 214.

43. Woody Allen, "The Scrolls," in *Without Feathers* (New York: Warner Books, 1976), p. 27.

44. Edmund Burke, *On the Sublime and the Beautiful*, Part 2, Section 2, in *The Harvard Classics*, Charles W. Eliot, ed. (New York: P. F. Collier & Son Corp., 1965), Vol. 24, pp. 49-50.

45. Eugène Ionesco, Preface to the Second Edition of *Rhinoceros*, in *Rhinocéros*, ed. R. Y. Ellison, S. C. Goding, and A. Raffanel (New York: Holt, Rinehart & Winston, 1976), p. xi.

46. Viktor E. Frankl, *Man's Search for Meaning* (New York: Washington Square Press, 1964), pp. 68 *ff.*

47. William Roper, More's son-in-law, was present at the execution and quotes More's last words to the executioner as, "Pluck up thy spirits, man, and be not afraid to do thine office, my neck is very short." See his "The Life of Sir Thomas More," in *The Harvard Classics*, Charles W. Eliot, ed. (New York: P. F. Collier & Son Co., 1965), Vol. 36, p. 134.

48. Kierkegaard, *Concluding Unscientific Postscript*, pp. 459-463.

49. Ibid., p. 466.

50. Ibid., p. 83.

51. See Will Durant, *The Story of Civilization* (New York: Simon & Schuster, 1935-), Vol. 2.

52. Kierkegaard, *Concluding Unscientific Postscript*, p. 42.

Conclusion

It is most interesting that Screwtape, experienced old devil that he is, should counsel his young nephew, Wormwood, to use humor as a temptation strategy. With consummate skill he distinguishes four causes of laughter: joy, fun, jokes, and flippancy. This last one he considers the best weapon against religion, for it requires no skill or exertion. Flippancy consists in implying without proof that there is something laughable about, say, virtue. Flippancy, says Screwtape, "builds up around a man the finest armour plating against the Enemy,"[1] for it makes people avoid any and every confrontation with what must be confronted on the grounds that it is funny. All you need is to "flip" and the threat is off.

Aside from this, Screwtape also makes the point that genuine humor is on the side of the angels and, therefore, must be avoided at all costs: it is "itself disgusting and a direct insult to the realism, dignity, and austerity of Hell."[2] Could this mean ironically that overly serious and proper people are in the service of the devil? This would make the reign of the Puritans in England during Cromwell's tenure the most devil-infested period in history. Not only did the Puritans denounce the theater, they "condemned festival jollities, ringing bells, gathering around the Maypole, drinking healths, playing cards . . . merrymaking, dancing, and games."[3]

THE RUMOR OF HUMOR

Many years ago, in a wonderful book, Peter Berger made the case that there are intimations of the supernatural or the transcendent all around us, only we often fail to notice them. He called these intimations "rumors," because they are not blared noisily from loudspeakers, but, rather, are whispered during quiet moments of wonder and contemplation, of which we don't seem to have an abundance today. Berger suggested that we call these "rumors" *"signals of transcendence* within the empirically given human situation," and that we look for them among *"prototypical human gestures,"* that is, "reiterated acts and experiences that appear to express essential aspects of man's being."[4] Among these "rumors" Berger included humor. Noting that all humor arises fundamentally from incongruity, discrepancy, and incommensurability, he postulated "one fundamental discrepancy from which all other comic discrepancies are derived — the discrepancy between man and universe."[5] Specifically, Berger claimed that *"the comic reflects the imprisonment of the human spirit in the world.*"[6] The comic perception, in other words, may look at this imprisonment and pretend it is suspended or over, and it does this in the joke, "every time it relativizes the seemingly rocklike necessities of the world."[7]

Ted Cohen agrees. In fact, when it comes to humor, he can state his point in the form of two complementary principles: "One, jokes cannot be the entire human response to death, or to anything else; two, any total response to death that does not include the possibility of jokes is less than a totally human response."[8] We all know this, which is the reason why we find jokes about death, tombs, and interments so funny. The Japanese poet Sengai wrote once that there are things that even the wise fail to see, while fools pick them up easily; for example, suddenly discovering life in the midst of death, like a lily blooming in a muddy field.[9]

> A man accused of murdering his wife was being tried. The prosecutor asked him, "Isn't it true that you would like to see your wife under six feet of earth?" "Four feet would be enough, sir," came the reply.

Here we may take the story of Captain Stormfield's visit to heaven as narrated by Mark Twain. Stormfield has been dead for some thirty years, flitting around the cosmos, when he finally finds himself before the gates of heaven with millions of other travelers. When his turn comes, the head clerk asks, in a businesslike way —

> "Well, quick! Where are you from?"
> "San Francisco," says I.
> "San Fran — *what*?" says he.
> "San Francisco."
> "Is it a planet?"[10]

Later on Captain Stormfield learns, to his surprise, that heaven is populated by all sorts of people with varied ideologies and persuasions, but he is told,

> Don't be alarmed. . . . That is the main charm of heaven — there's all kinds here — which wouldn't be the case if you let the preachers tell it. Anybody can find the sort he prefers, here, and he just lets the others alone, and they let him alone. When the Deity builds a heaven, it is built right, and on a liberal plan.[11]

All this goes to show that there cannot be an incompatibility between humor and faith.[12] Or, if one wishes to push the point, that the incompatibility of humor and faith is itself comic and should be a cause for serious laughter.

THE SCHOOL OF HUMOR

We saw in the previous chapter that in *Steppenwolf* Hesse set the Magic Theater as "a school of humor," a place to learn to laugh. In it there were multiple stages on which the various "lessons" were enacted, at times with unusual starkness and realism. For our times, a "school of humor" would include several special classrooms in which different topics relating to humor would be taught. Some of the lessons might look like this:

THE FEAST OF FOOLS

During the medieval era there flourished in parts of Europe a holiday known as the Feast of Fools. On that colorful occasion, usually celebrated about January first, even ordinary pious priests and serious townsfolk donned bawdy masks, sang outrageous ditties, and generally kept the whole world awake with revelry and satire. Minor clerics painted their faces, strutted about in the robes of their superiors, and mocked the stately rituals of church and court. Sometimes a Lord of Misrule, a Mock King, or a Boy Bishop was elected to preside over the events. In some places the Boy Bishop even celebrated a parody mass. During the Feast of Fools, no custom or convention was immune to ridicule and even the highest personages of the realm could expect to be lampooned.

The Feast of Fools was never popular with the higher-ups. It was constantly condemned and criticized. But despite the efforts of fidgety ecclesiastics and an outright condemnation by the Council of Basel in 1431, the Feast of Fools survived until the sixteenth century. Then in the age of Reformation and Counter-Reformation it gradually died out. Its faint shade still persists in the pranks and revelry of Halloween and New Year's Eve.[13]

HOW WARS START

One morning . . . Reldresal, Principal Secretary (as they style him) of Private Affairs, came to my house . . . and desired I would give him an hour's audience; which I readily consented to. . . . He began with compliments . . . but, however, added . . . We are threatened with an invasion from the island of Blefuscu, which is the other great empire of the universe, almost as large and powerful as this of his Majesty. For . . . our histories of six thousand moons make no mention of any other regions, than the two great empires of Lilliput and Blefuscu. Which two mighty powers have . . . been engaged in a most obstinate war for six and thirty moons past. It began upon the following occasion. It is allowed on all hands, that the primitive way of breaking eggs before we eat them, was upon the larger end: but his present Majesty's grand-father, while he was a boy, going to eat an egg, and breaking it according to the ancient practice, happened to cut one of his fingers. Whereupon the emperor his father, published an edict, commanding all his subjects, upon great penalties, to break the smaller ends of their eggs. The people so highly resented this law, that our histories tell us, there have been six rebellions raised on that account; wherein one emperor lost his life, and another his crown. These civil commotions were constantly fomented by the monarchs of Blefuscu; and when they were quelled, the exiles always fled for refuge to that empire. It is computed, that eleven thousand persons have, at several times, suffered death, rather than submit to break their eggs at the smaller end. . . . Now the Big-Endian exiles have found so much credit in the Emperor of Blefuscu's court . . . that they have now equipped a numerous fleet, and are just preparing to make a descent upon us.[14]

THE LAST DANCE

Before he was arrested . . . [Jesus] assembled us all and said, "Before I am delivered to them, let us sing a hymn to the Father. . . ." So he told us to form a circle, holding one another's hands, and himself stood in the middle and said, "Answer 'Amen' to me." So he began to sing the hymn and to say:

"Glory be to thee, Father" [he said].
And we circled round him and answered him,   — "Amen."

. . . .
"We praise thee, Father:
  We thank thee, Light:
  In whom darkness dwelleth not."   — "Amen."

. . . .
[Then] Grace danced.
  "I will pipe;
  Dance, all of you."   — "Amen."

. . . .
"To the Universe belongs the dancer."   — "Amen."
"He who does not dance
 does not know what happens."   — "Amen."

. . . .
"Now, if you follow my dance,
  you will see yourselves in me who am speaking,
  and when you have seen what I do,
  keep silence about my mysteries.
  You who dance, consider what I do,
  for yours is this passion of Man
  which I am to suffer.
  For you by no means could have understood
  what you suffer unless to you as Logos
  I had been sent by the Father.

. . . .
"As for me, if you would understand what I was:
  By the word I mocked all things,
  and I was not mocked at all,
  I leaped for joy;
  but strive to understand the whole,
  and when you have understood it, say,
  'Glory be to thee, Father.' "

"Say again with me:
  'Glory be to thee, Father,
  Glory be to thee, Word,
  Glory be to thee, Spirit.' "   — "Amen."

After the Lord had so danced with us, my beloved, he went out. And we were like men amazed or fast asleep.[15]

TEACHING AND LEARNING

A disciple approached Kendo and asked: "Master, teach me to teach."

Kendo answered: "Teaching cannot be taught. No one can teach another how to teach."

The disciple insisted: "If teaching cannot be taught, why are there so many people seeking to be taught how to teach?"

Kendo replied: "Precisely because teaching cannot be taught!"[16]

TO LEARN TO LAUGH

We saw in Chapter 6 that for paradox to eventuate in laughter, the humorous attitude must supervene. The humorous attitude is the ability or capacity to transport oneself beyond the confines of the paradox and dissolve into smile or burst into laughter. Kant thought that this humorous attitude was a talent, that is, an inborn capacity that some people possess which others do not, or that some possess to a greater degree; after all, some people invent the joke while most of us are able to laugh only once the joke is told. One could say, paraphrasing Michelangelo, that the world is composed of three classes of people, those who laugh, those who laugh when prompted, and those who do not laugh.

It would seem, then, that if, as was pointed out above, it is always possible to learn to laugh, there must be in us — or at least in most of us — an inchoate capacity for humor that can be developed. But matters are not as simple as that, because our experiences in life are multiple and often lead to the formation of attitudes that are quite inimical to laughter. Buber claims that "each of us is encased in an armour whose task is to ward off signs,"[17] those promptings of the universe around us, the myriad paradoxes we encounter in our daily living. "But the risk is too dangerous for us,"[18] so we learn, instead, not to listen, not to feel addressed, and, consequently, not to laugh. After years of cowering we no longer notice we slither through life instead of striding with valor and confidence in the face of paradox. For it often takes courage to laugh.

This is a major reason why we must learn to laugh, lest our lives be lived at the margin, as it were. Nietzsche claimed that Jesus died too early, before he had learned "to live and to love the earth — and laughter too,"[19] though perhaps this judgment is based on what Jesus's followers wrote after his death; but the same verdict can be passed on too many of us.

If humor can be learned — must be learned — what is it that is learned? What is it that allows us to view the paradox and laugh? Kant says it is the imagination. What is the imagination? The imagination, says Sartre, "is but a certain way in which consciousness takes aim on its object."[20] This means that to imagine something, something must be denied relationally, that is, in the very act and in reference to the very object. If nothing were denied, nothing could be imagined: the mind would merely photograph. To imagine is to claim that what is denied in the object is recovered in the image. Sartre, again: "If negation is the unconditioned principle of all imagination, reciprocally it can never take place except by and in an act of imagination. What is denied must be imagined."[21] Imagination, then, allows us to deny the sting of the paradox — to act as if it were not there — and to imagine the joke, which itself preserves the paradox, but as imagined. Imagination empowers us to free ourselves from the clutches of the paradoxical and to conceive a solution that has value in the "never-never" land of the joke. The imagination, Sartre, said, "is the mind itself in so far as it is free."[22]

How can one develop the imagination so that it may ground the sense of humor we all must learn? By freeing our thinking from the exaggerated objectivity of our current situation. Children, as Piaget has shown, enjoy a certain predominance of the imaginative, the "assimilative," over the objective, the "accommodative,"[23] and this is why they play. As we grow up, the emphasis shifts to the objective, for we need to tally dollars and cents, balance checkbooks, predict tornadoes, cure cancer, and fight bioterrorism. But too often we forget that the objective is only half of life and we neglect to savor the subjective and and foster it again in ourselves. True, there has been a slight change in this, for we have grown more and more interested in games of all sorts, in the theater, and in music, but we still need to devote more time and energy to the reading of good literature, to the fruits of art in our museums, and to the cultivation of genuine friendships. Above all, we need to stop pushing children too early into activities, such as reading, which begin to tilt their playfulness too soon toward the serious business of schooling. We need to understand more deeply that the imagination is not peripheral to life but, as William Blake claimed — and he should know! — "it is the Human Existence itself."[24]

Mark Twain has preserved these words of Eve in her diary:

> I feel like an experiment, I feel exactly like an experiment; it would be impossible for a person to feel more like an experiment than I do, and so I am coming to feel convinced that that is what I *am* — an experiment; just an experiment, and nothing more.[25]

This is what *we* are, experiments in search of direction, but with a sense of humor!

EPILOGUE

In the literature on humor and faith there is an allegory that, because of its insight and simplicity, has been retold again and again throughout the centuries. It is indeed a pearl of great price. It clothes with beautiful imagery the profound understanding of the need for a faith that is both steadfast and humorous in the face of paradox.

The allegory is built around a story in *Genesis* 26:8. Because of a great famine, Isaac and Rebecca, his wife, went to live in the land of the Philistines. They were well received by the people and by their ruler, King Abimelech. Some men of the palace asked Isaac about the woman with him, for she was very beautiful. Fearing that someone might kill him in order to possess Rebecca, Isaac responded that she was his sister, since the brother-sister bond was deemed very sacred among the people. One afternoon some time later, King Abimelech was looking out of his window when he saw Isaac playing with Rebecca. "Abimelech saw Isaac fondling his wife Rebecca." Here the allegory begins.

Isaac means "laughter" in Hebrew, and Rebecca means "perseverance," "steadfastness." Perseverance and laughter are seen playing with each other; and it is thus that the King discovers that they are husband and wife.

Philo of Alexandria was the first one to use the allegory for the union of steadfastness and humor in faith. He wrote:

> True wisdom is never scowling or severe, nor is it full of worry and misgivings. On the contrary, it is gay and friendly, full of heartsease and joy. These qualities have moved many a man to witty jest; yet behind such jesting countertones of gravity and dignity must be audible, like the music of a well-tuned lyre. According

to Moses, the end of wisdom is sport and laughter, not after the manner of the childish and unthinking, but after that of those who have grown gray, if not in years, at least in the good disposition of their souls. . . . Here we have Isaac, whose name means "laughter," for whom it is only right and proper to play with "perseverance," as the Hebrews call Rebecca. Yet such divine jesting of the soul must not be witnessed by any ordinary man, but only by a king . . . Abimelech. The King looked through the window, by which is meant the soul's eye which sees into the open light beyond, and beheld Isaac playing with Rebecca his wife. For what could be more fitting for a wise man than to play, to be merry and glad hearted, when perseverance in the good is at his side?[26]

Some one hundred years later Clement of Alexandria (*ca.* 215) was so overpowered by the beauty of this allegory that he sang a hymn to the unity of seriousness and laughter, perseverance and humor, in faith:

> Oh, the wisdom of this playing!
> Perseverance the playmate of laughter —
> And all witnessed by the King!
> Joyful is the spirit of those
> Who are children in Christ
> And order their lives with patient perseverance.
> This is indeed the playing of the children of God![27]

No words could be more fitting to end this little treatise on the religious significance of humor.

NOTES

1. C. S. Lewis, *The Screwtape Letters* (New York: Macmillan, 1962), p. 52.
2. Ibid., p. 50.
3. Will and Ariel Durant, *The Age of Reason Begins* (New York: Simon & Schuster, 1961), p. 191.
4. Peter L. Berger, *A Rumor of Angels* (Garden City, NY: Doubleday & Co., 1969), pp. 65-66.
5. Ibid., p. 87.
6. Ibid.
7. Ibid., p. 89.
8. Ted Cohen, *Jokes. Philosophical Thoughts on Joking Matters* (Chicago: The University of Chicago Press, 1999), p. 70.
9. Sengai, quoted in Daisetz T. Suzuki, *Sengai, the Zen Master* (New York: The New York Graphic Society, 1971), p. 134, in Conrad Hyers, "The Smile of Truth," *Parabola* 12:4 (November, 1987), p. 57.
10. Mark Twain, "Captain Stormfield's Visit to Heaven," in *The Family Mark Twain* (New York: Harper & Row, 1972), Vol. 2, p. 1253.
11. Ibid., p. 1267.
12. Cohen, *Jokes*, p. 54.
13. Harvey Cox, *The Feast of Fools: A Theological Essay on Festivity and Fantasy* (New York: Harper Colophon Books, 1969), p. 3.
14. Jonathan Swift, *Gulliver's Travels*, Part I, Chapter 4, in *Great Books of the Western World*, Robert M. Hutchins, ed. (Chicago: Encyclopedia Britannica, 1952), Vol. 36, pp. 21-23.

15. *Acts of John* 95-97, in *New Testament Apocrypha*, Edgar Hennecke and Wilhelm Schneemelcher, eds. (Philadelphia: The Westminster Press, 1964), pp. 227-232.

16. Ignacio L. Götz, *Zen and the Art of Teaching* (Westbury, NY: J. L. Wilkerson Publishing Co., 1988), p. 150.

17. Martin Buber, *Between Man and Man* (New York: Macmillan, 1967), p. 10.

18. Ibid.

19. Friedrich Nietzsche, *Thus Spoke Zarathustra* (New York: Viking, 1966), Part I, 21, p. 73.

20. Jean-Paul Sartre, *The Imagination* (Ann Arbor: The University of Michigan Press, 1972), p. 135.

21. Jean-Paul Sartre, *The Psychology of Imagination* (Secaucus, NJ: Citadel Press, 1972), pp. 272-273.

22. Ibid., p. 270. Also Ignacio L. Götz, *Creativity: Theoretical and Socio-Cosmic Reflections* (Washington, DC: University Press of America, 1978), Chapter 1.

23. Jean Piaget, *The Origins of Intelligence in Children* (New York: W. W. Norton & Co., 1963), p. 6.

24. William Blake, *Milton*, Book II, 32, 32, in *Complete Writings*, Geoffrey Keynes, ed. (London: Oxford University Press, 1969).

25. Mark Twain, "Eve's Diary," in *The Family Mark Twain* (New York: Harper & Row, 1972), Vol. 2, p. 1115.

26. Philo of Alexandria, *De Plantatione*, XL, 167-170, in *Works of Philo, Complete and Unabridged*, C. D. Yonge, transl. (Peabody, MA: Hendrickson Pub., 1993).

27. Clement of Alexandria, *Paedagogus* I, 5, 21, 3-4, Simon P. Wood, transl. (New York: Fathers of the Church, Inc., 1954).

Bibliography

Adams, Henry. *The Education of Henry Adams*. New York: The Modern Library, 1931.

Adorno, Theodor. *Negative Dialectics*. New York: Seabury Press, 1973.

Aflākī, Shams ad-Dīn Ahmad. *Manāqib al-'Ārifīn* (Virtues of the Knowers). Tehran: Duniyā-yi Kitāb, 1983, in *Early Islamic Mysticism*, Michael A. Sells, ed. New York: Paulist Press, 1996.

Alighieri, Dante. *The Divine Comedy*, in *Great Books of the Western World*, Robert M. Hutchins, ed. Chicago: Encyclopedia Britannica, 1952.

Allen, Woody. *Without Feathers*. New York: Warner Books, 1976.

Anastas, Benjamin. *An Underachiever's Diary*. New York: The Dial Press, 1998.

Anselm, Saint. *Proslogium; Monologium; An Appendix on Behalf of the Fool by Gaunilon; and Cur Deus Homo*, Sidney Norton Dean, trans. Chicago: The Open Court Publishing Co., 1939.

Aquinas, St. Thomas. *Opera Omnia*, E. Fretté and P. Maré, eds. Paris: 1872-1880.

Arendt, Hannah. *The Human Condition*. New York: Doubleday Anchor, 1959.

———. *On Violence*. New York: Harcourt, Brace & World, Inc., 1970.

Aristotle. *The Complete Works of Aristotle*, Jonathan Barnes, ed. 2 vols. Princeton, NJ: Princeton University Press, 1984.

Āryanāgārjunīyam Madhyamika shāstram (Vāranāsī: Bauddhabhāratī, 1983).

Ashtasāhasrikā Prajñāpāramitā, Edward Conze, trans. Calcutta: Asiatic Society, 1970.

'Attār, Farīduddīn. *Mantiq al-Tayr* (The Conference of the Birds). Boston: Shambhala, 1993.

———. *Tadhikrat al-'Awliyā'*, Muhammad Istislāmī, ed. Tehran: Zavvār, 1967, re-edited by Nāsir Hayyirī. Tehran: Intishārāt-I Gulshā'ī, 1982, in *Early Islamic Mysticism*, Michael A. Sells, ed. New York: Paulist Press, 1996.

Augustine, St. *Opera Omnia*, in *Patrologiae cursus completus*, Series Latina, J. P. Migne, ed. Paris: Garnier, 1844-1855.

Awliyā, Nizam Ad-dīn.. *Morals of the Heart (Fawa 'id al-Fu'ad)*, Bruce B. Lawrence, trans. New York: Paulist Press, 1992.

Awn, Peter J. *Satan's Tragedy and Redemption: Iblīs in Sufi Psychology*. Leiden: E. J. Brill, 1983.

Ayer, Alfred Jules. *Language, Truth and Logic*. New York: Dover Publications, Inc., n.d.

Balthasar, Hans Urs von, S. J. *Prayer*. New York: Paulist Press, 1967.

Barnes, Timothy. *Tertullian. A Historical and Literary Study*. Oxford: Oxford University Press, 1971.

Barth, Karl. *The Epistle to the Romans*. London: Oxford University Press, 1933.

———. *Fides quaerens intellectum: Anselms Bewis der Existenz Gottes*. Munich: Kaiser Verlag, 1931.

Beattie, James. *Essays*. Edinburgh: William Greech, 1776.

Berger, Peter. *A Rumor of Angels*. Garden City, NY: Doubleday & Co., 1969.

Bergson, Henri. "Laughter," in *Comedy*, Wylie Sypher, ed. New York: Doubleday Anchor, 1956.

Berlinerblau, Jacques. "Official Religion and Popular Religion in Pre-Exilic Ancient Israel." <http://bibleinterp.com/articles/berlinerblau.htm>

Blake, William. *Milton*, in *Complete Writings*, Geoffrey Keynes, ed. London: Oxford University Press, 1969.

Bloch, Ernst. *The Principle of Hope*. Cambridge, MA: MIT Press, 1986.

Bonhoeffer, Dietrich. *Letters and Papers from Prison*. New York: Macmillan, 1962.

Boolos, George, "Gödel's Second Incompleteness Theorem Explained in Words of One Syllable." *Mind* 103:409 (January, 1994): 1-3.

Bradbury, Ray. *Fahrenheit 451*. New York: Ballantine Books, 1991.

Brewer, Mary Ann. "Tío Conejo and the Hurricane," in *Treasury of North American Folk Tales*, Catherine Peck, ed. New York: Quality Paperback Book Club, 1998.

Brodwin, Stanley. "The Humor of the Absurd: Mark Twain's Adamic Diaries." *Criticism* 14:1 (Winter, 1972).

Bronowski, Jacob, "The Logic of the Mind." *American Scientist* 54:1 (March, 1966): 4-5.

Brown, Norman O. "Apocalypse: The Place of Mystery in the Life of the Mind," in *The Movement Toward a New America*, Mitchell Goodman, ed. New York: Alfred Knopf, 1970.

Buber, Martin. *Between Man and Man*. New York: Macmillan, 1967.

Al-Bukhārī. *Kitāb al-Jāmi'al-Sahīh*, Krehl and Juynboll, trans. and eds. Leyden, 1868-1908.

Burke, Edmund. *On the Sublime and the Beautiful*, in *The Harvard Classics*, Charles W. Eliot, ed. New York: P. F. Collier & Son Corp., 1965.

Burns, Robert. *The Jolly Beggars*, in *The Harvard Classics*, Charles W. Eliot, ed. New York: P. F. Collier & Son, Co., 1965.

Bushnaq, Inea, trans. & ed. *Arab Folktales*. New York: Pantheon Books, 1986.

Camus, Albert. *Caligula and Three Other Plays*. New York: Vintage, 1958.

———. *Exile and the Kingdom*. New York: Vintage, 1958.

———. *Lyrical and Critical Essays*, Philip Thody, ed. New York: Vintage, 1970.

———. *The Myth of Sisyphus*. New York: Vintage, 1955.

———. *The Plague*. New York: The Modern Library, 1948.

———. "Trois interviews," in *Essais*, Roger Quilliot, ed. Paris: Éditions Gallimard, 1965.

Cervigni, Dino S., "Dante's Lucifer: the Denial of the Word." <http://www.brown.edu/departments/italian_studies/ld/numbers/03/cervigni.html>

Chadwick, Henry. *Early Christian Thought and the Classical Tradition*. New York: Oxford University Press, 1966.

Chapman, Tony and Foot, Hugh, ed. *Humor and Laughter: Theory, Research, and Application*. London: J. Wiley & Sons, 1976.

Charles, R. H., trans. and ed. *The Apocrypha and Pseudepigrapha of the Old Testament in English*. Oxford: Clarendon Press, 1913/1969.

Chesterton, G. K., "Lucifer or the Root of Evil," 1929. <http://www.abcog.org/pride.htm>

Chilton, Bruce. *Rabbi Jesus. An Intimate Biography*. New York: Doubleday, 2000.

Chittick, William C. and Murata, Sachiko. *The Vision of Islam*. New York: Paragon House, 1994.

Chrysostom, St. John. *Homilies on the Gospel of Mattew*. New York: Catholic University of America Press, 1998; reprint of the Post-Nicene Christian Library edition of 1888.

Chuang-tzu. *The Complete Works of Chuang-tzu*, Burton Watson, trans. New York: Columbia University Press, 1968.

Cicero, Marcus Tullius. *Oeuvres Complètes*. Paris: Firmin-Didot, 1881.

Clement of Alexandria. *Paedagogus* (Christ the Educator), Simon P. Wood, trans. New York: Fathers of the Church, Inc., 1954.

Cohen, Ted. *Jokes: Philosophical Thoughts on Joking Matters*. Chicago: The University of Chicago Press, 1999.

Confucius. *The Analects*, Arthur Waley, trans. New York: Vintage, 1938.

Cox, Harvey. *The Feast of Fools: A Theological Essay on Festivity and Fantasy*. New York: Harper Colophon Books, 1969.

Cragg, Kenneth. *The House of Islam*, 2nd ed. Belmont, CA: Wadsworth Publishing Co., 1975.

Dart, John. *The Jesus of Heresy and History: The Discovery and Significance of the Nag Hammadi Gnostic Library in English*. New York: Harper & Row, 1988.

De Bono, Edward. *Lateral Thinking: Creativity Step by Step*. New York: Harper Colophon, 1970.

Décarie, V. "Le paradoxe de Tertullien." *Vigiliae Christianae* 15 (1961).

Delbanco, Andrew. *The Death of Satan*. New York: Farrar, Straus & Giroux, 1995.

De Lubac, Henri, S. J. *Catholicism*. New York: Mentor-Omega, 1964.

De Vitray-Meyerovitch, Eva. *Rūmī and Sufism*. Sausalito, CA: The Post-Apollo Press, 1987.

Durant, Will. *The Story of Civilization*. New York: Simon & Schuster, 1935-.

Durant, Will and Ariel. *The Age of Reason Begins*. New York: Simon & Schuster, 1961.

Durkheim, Emile. *Suicide*. New York: The Free Press, 1951.

Eastman, Max. *Enjoyment of Laughter*. New York: Simon & Schuster, 1936.

Eco, Umberto. *The Name of the Rose*. New York: Warner Books, 1984.

El Hakim, Tewfik. "The Martyr," in *Arabic Writing Today: The Short Story*, Mahmoud Manzalaoui, ed. Cairo: American Research Center in Egypt, 1968.

Emerson, Ralph Waldo. *Emerson's Essays*. New York: Books Inc., n. d.

Erasmus of Rotterdam, Desiderius. *Praise of Folly*. London: Penguin Books, 1971.

Erdoes, Richard, and Ortiz, Alfonso, eds. *American Indian Myths and Legends*. New York: Pantheon Books, 1984.

Eusebius. *Historia Ecclesiastica* (The History of the Church). New York: Barnes & Noble, 1995.

Ferlinghetti, Lawrence. *A Coney Island of the Mind*. New York: New Directions, 1958.

Fitzmeyer, Joseph A., S. J. *The Gospel According to Luke*. Garden City, NY: Doubleday & Co., Inc., 1985.

Forman, Robert K. C., ed. *The Problem of Pure Consciousness*. New York: Oxford University Press, 1990.

Fowler, James W. *Stages of Faith*. San Francisco: Harper & Row, 1981.

Frankl, Viktor E. *Man's Search for Meaning*. New York: Washington Square Press, 1964.

Freud, Sigmund. *The Basic Writings of Sigmund Freud*, A. A. Brill, ed. New York: The Modern Library, 1938.

————. *Collected Works*, Standard Edition, James Strachey, ed. London: Hogarth Press, 1961.

Friedländer, Paul. *Plato*. New York: Pantheon Books, 1958.

Friedman, Maurice. *Problematic Rebel*, revised ed. Chicago: The University of Chicago Press, 1970.

Gabaldón Márques, Joaquín and Anzola-Carrillo, Antonio José. *La risa de Sócrates y otras risas*. Buenos Aires: Imprenta López, 1962.

Gelven, Michael. *Spirit and Existence*. Notre Dame, IN: University of Notre Dame Press, 1990.

Gensler, Harry. *Gödel's Theorem Simplified*. Lanham, MD: University Press of America, 1984.

Gerassi, John, ed. *Venceremos! The Speeches and Writings of Ernesto Che Guevara*. New York: Simon & Schuster, 1968.

Al-Ghazālī, Mohammed. *Al-Munqidh min al-dalāl* (Deliverance from Error), trans. by Montgomery Watt as *The Faith and Practice of Al-Ghazali*. London: George, Allen & Unwin, Ltd., 1953.

————. *Ihya' 'ulum al-din*. Beirut: Dar al-Hadi, 1992.

Ginza: Der Schatz oder das Grosse Buch der Mandäer, M. Lidzbarski, trans. Göttingen, 1925.

Glassé, Cyril. *Concise Encyclopedia of Islam*. San Francisco: Harper & Row, 1989.

Gödel, Kurt, "Über formal unentschiedbare Sätze der *Principia Mathematica* und verwandter Systeme, I." *Monatshefte für Mathematik und Physik* 38 (1931): 173-198.

Goethe, Johann W. von. *Goethes Werke*. 14 vols. Hamburg: Christian Wegner Verlag, 1948.

Golding, William. *Lord of the Flies*. New York: Capricorn Books, 1959.

Götz, Ignacio L. *Creativity: Theoretical and Socio-Cosmic Reflections*. Washington, DC: University Press of America, 1978.

————. "Unamuno: Paradox and Humor," in *Selected Proceedings of the* Singularidad y Trascendencia *Conference*, Nora de Marval-McNair, ed. Boulder, CO: University of Colorado, 1990.

————. *Zen and the Art of Teaching*. Westbury, NY: J. L. Wilkerson Publishing Co., 1988.

Gray, J. Glenn. *On Understanding Violence Philosophically and Other Essays*. New York: Harper Torchbooks, 1970.

Gregory of Nazianzus. *Opera*, in *Patrologiae Cursus Completus*, Series Graeca, J. P. Migne, ed. Paris: Garnier, 1857-1866.

Gur-Ze'ev, Ilan. "Philosophy of Peace Education in a Postmodern Era." *Educational Theory* 51:3 (Summer 2001): 315-336.

Al-Hallāj, Al-Husayn ibn Mansūr. *TāSīn of before-time and ambiguity*, in *Early Islamic Mysticism*, Michael A. Sells, trans. and ed. New York: Paulist Press, 1996.

Hare, Richard M. *Freedom and Reason*. New York: Oxford University Press, 1965.

Harris, Paul, ed. *The Fire of Silence and Stillness*. Springfield, IL: Templegate Publishers, 1997.

Hassan, Nasra, "An Arsenal of Believers," *The New Yorker*, November 19, 2001.

Hegel, G.W.F. *The Phenomenology of Mind*, in *Great Books of the Western World*, Robert M. Hutchins, ed. Chicago: Encyclopaedia Britannica, 1952.

Heidegger, Martin. *An Introduction to Metaphysics*. New York: Doubleday Anchor Books, 1961.

Hennecke, Edgar and Schneemelcher, Wilhelm, eds. *New Testament Apocrypha*. Philadelphia: The Westminster Press, 1964.

Herhardt, Göram. "Incongruity and Funniness: Toward a New Descriptive Model," in *Humor and Laughter: Theory, Research, and Application*, Tony Chapman and Hugh Foot, eds. London: J. Wiley & Sons, 1976.

Heschel, Abraham. *Israel: An Echo of God*. New York: Farrar, Straus & Giroux, 1969.

Hesse, Hermann. *The Glass Bead Game*. New York: Henry Holt & Co., Inc., 1990.

————. *The Journey to the East*, Hilda Rosner, trans. London: P. Owen, 1964.

————. *Steppenwolf*. New York: Holt, Rinehart & Winston, 1963.

Hobbes, Thomas. *Leviathan*, in *Great Books of the Western World*, Robert M. Hutchins, ed. Chicago: Encyclopedia Britannica, 1952.

Hoffer, Eric. *The True Believer*. New York: Harper & Row, 1951.

Hofstadter, Douglas R. *Gödel, Escher, Bach.* New York: Basic Books, 1979.

Horace, Quintus. *The Satires, Epistles and Ars Poetica,* H. Rushton Fairclough, trans. *The Loeb Classical Library.* Cambridge, MA: Harvard University Press, 1926.

Hughes, Patrick, and Brecht, George. *Vicious Circles and Infinity.* New York: Penguin Books, 1979.

Huizinga, Johan. *Homo Ludens: A Study of the Play-Element in Culture.* Boston: Beacon Press, 1966.

Huxley, Aldous. *The Devils of Loudun.* New York: Harper Colophon, 1965.

Hyde, Lewis. *Trickster Makes This World.* New York: Farrar, Straus & Giroux, 1998.

Hyers, M. Conrad. "The Dialectic of the Sacred and the Comic." *Cross Currents* 19 (Winter 1969): 72-79.

———. "The Smile of Truth." *Parabola* 12:4 (November, 1987).

The Iliad, in *Great Books of the Western World,* Robert M. Hutchins, ed. Chicago: Encyclopedia Britannica, 1952.

Ionesco, Eugène. *Rhinocéros,* R. Y. Ellison, S. C. Goding, and A. Raffanel, eds. New York: Holt, Rinehart & Winston, 1976.

Jacobs, Louis. *Faith.* New York: Basic Books, 1968.

James, William. *Essays in Pragmatism.* New York: Hafner Publishing Co., 1966.

———. *The Principles of Psychology,* in *Great Books of the Western World,* Robert M. Hutchins, ed. Chicago: Encyclopaedia Britannica, 1952.

———. *The Varieties of Religious Experience.* New York: Mentor, 1964.

Jaspers, Karl. *Nietzsche.* Chicago: Gateway Editions, 1969.

———. *Philosophy.* Chicago: The University of Chicago Press, 1969.

———. *Reason and Existenz.* New York: The Noonday Press, 1957.

Jonas, Hans. *Gnosticism.* Boston: Beacon Press, 1963.

Joyce, James. *A Portrait of the Artist as a Young Man.* New York: The Viking Press, 1958.

Kamran, Gilani. *Ana al-Haqq Reconsidered.* Lahore: Naqsh-e-Awwal Kitab Ghar, 1398/ 1987.

Kant, Immanuel. *Beobachtungen über des Schönen und Erhabenen* [1764], in *Immanuel Kants Werke,* Ernst Cassirer, ed. Berlin: Bruno Cassirer, 1922-1923.

———. *Critique of Judgment,* in *Great Books of the Western World,* Robert M. Hutchins, ed. Chicago: Encyclopedia Britannica, 1952.

Kapleau, Philip. *The Three Pillars of Zen.* Boston: Beacon Press, 1966.

Kaufmann, Walter. *Critique of Religion and Philosophy.* New York: Anchor Books, 1961.

———. *The Faith of a Heretic.* New York: Anchor Books, 1963.

———. *Without Guilt and Justice.* New York: Dell Publishing Co., Inc., 1973.

Kendall, Elaine. *The Happy Mediocrity.* New York: G. P. Putnam's Sons, 1971.

Kierkegaard, Søren. *The Concept of Irony.* Bloomington, IN: Indiana University Press, 1968.

———. *Concluding Unscientific Postscript.* Princeton, NJ: Princeton University Press, 1968.

———. *Fear and Trembling* and *The Sickness Unto Death.* Garden City, NY: Doubleday Anchor, 1955.

———. *The Journals.* Oxford: Oxford University Press, 1938.

———. *Philosophical Fragments.* Princeton, NJ: Princeton University Press, 1962.

———. *The Present Age.* New York: Harper Torchbooks, 1962.

———. *Stages on Life's Way.* Princeton: Princeton University Press, 1988.

Kipling, Rudyard. *Kim.* London: Macmillan & Co., Ltd., n. d.

Kleene, Stephen C. *Introduction to Mathematics.* New York: D. Van Nostrand Co., Inc., 1952.

Koestler, Arthur. *The Act of Creation.* New York: Macmillan, 1964.

Kris, Ernst. "Ego Development and the Comic." *International Journal of Psychoanalysis* 19 (1938): 77-90.

Kuhn, Thomas S. *The Structure of Scientific Revolutions*. Chicago: The University of Chicago Press, 1970.

Kuschel, Harl-Josef. *Laughter: A Theological Reflection*. New York: Continuum, 1994.

La Fave, Lawrence, Haddad, Jay, and Maesen, William A. "Superiority, Enhanced Self-esteem, and Perceived Incongruity Humor Theory," in *Humor and Laughter: Theory, Research, and Application*, Tony Chapman and Hugh Foot, eds. London: J. Wiley & Sons, 1976.

Lao-tzu. *Lao-tzu Te-Tao Ching*, Robert G. Henricks, trans. and ed. New York: Ballantine Books, 1989.

Lehmann, Paul. *Ethics in a Christian Context*. New York: Harper & Row, 1963.

Levi, Primo. *The Drowned and the Saved*. New York: Vintage, 1989.

Lewis, C. S. *The Screwtape Letters*. New York: Macmillan, 1962.

Liber usualis, edited by the Benedictines of Solesmes. Tournai, Belgium: Desclée & Co., 1961.

Lilla, Mark. "The Lure of Syracuse." *The New York Review of Books*, September 20, 2001.

Lonergan, Bernard J.F., S. J. *Insight: A Study of Human Understanding*. New York: Philosophical Library, 1967.

Mackey, Louis. "Søren Kierkegaard: The Poetry of Inwardness," in *Existential Philosophers: Kierkegaard to Merleau-Ponty*, George Alfred Schrader, ed. New York: McGraw-Hill Book Co., 1967.

Marcel, Gabriel. *Homo Viator*. New York: Harper Torchbooks, 1962.

Marcuse, Herbert. *One-Dimensional Man*. Boston: Beacon Press, 1964.

———. "Repressive Tolerance," in *A Critique of Pure Tolerance*, Robert Paul Wolff *et al*. Boston: Beacon Press, 1969.

Maréchal, Josef, S. J. *Studies in the Psychology of the Mystics*. Albany, NY: Magi Books, Inc., 1964.

Maritain, Jacques. *Man and the State*. Chicago: The University of Chicago Press, 1961.

Massignon, Louis. *The Passion of al-Hallaj: Mystic and Martyr of Islam*. Princeton, NJ: Princeton University Press, 1982.

Mayotte, Ricky Alan. *The Complete Jesus*. South Royalton, VT: Steerforth Press, 1997.

Mazar, Amihai, and Stern, Ephraim. *Archaeology of the Land of the Bible*. 2 vols. New York: Doubleday, 1990 and 2001.

McGhee, Paul. "Development of the Humor Response." *Psychological Bulletin* 76:5 (1971): 328-348.

Meeks, Wayne A. *The Origins of Christian Morality*. New Haven, CT: Yale University Press, 1993.

Merleau-Ponty, Maurice. *Humanism and Terror*. Boston: Beacon Press, 1969.

Meyer, Wilhelm, ed. "Vita Adae et Evae." *Abhandlugen der Bayerschen Akademie der Wissenschaften: Philosophisch-philologische Classe* 14 (1878): 187-250.

Miles, Jack. *Christ: A Crisis in the Life of God*. New York: Alfred A. Knopf, 2001.

Milton, John. *Paradise Lost*, in *Great Books of the Western World*, Robert M. Hutchins, ed. Chicago: Encyclopedia Britannica, 1952.

———. *Samson Agonistes*, in *Great Books of the Western World*, Robert M. Hutchins, ed. Chicago: Encyclopedia Britannica, 1952.

Moltmann, Jürgen. *Theology of Hope*. New York: Harper & Row, 1967.

Monro, David H. *Argument of Laughter*. Notre Dame, IN: University of Notre Dame Press, 1963.

Montaigne, Michel Eyquem de. *The Essays*, in *Great Books of the Western World*, Robert M. Hutchins, ed. Chicago: Encyclopedia Britannica, 1952.

More, Sir Thomas. *Utopia*, in *The Harvard Classics*, Charles W. Eliot, ed. New York: P. F. Collier & Son, Co., 1965.

Moscher, Franz M. *Christian Prayer*. New York: B. Herder Book Co., 1962.

Nietzsche, Friedrich. *The Birth of Tragedy*. New York: Vintage, 1967.

————. *The Will to Power*, W. Kaufmann and R. J. Hollingdale, trans. New York: Random House, 1967.

————. *Ecce Homo*. New York: Vintage, 1967.

————. *Schopenhauer as Educator*, James W. Hilsheim and Malcom R. Simpson, trans. Chicago: Henry Regnery Co., 1965.

————. *Thus Spoke Zarathustra*. New York: Viking, 1966.

————. *Twilight of the Idols*. New York: Vintage, 1968.

The Odyssey, in *Great Books of the Western World*, Robert M. Hutchins, ed. Chicago: Encyclopaedia Britannica, 1952.

Ortega y Gasset, José. *Man and Crisis*. New York: W. W. Norton & Co., 1962.

————. *Mission of the University*. New York: W. W. Norton & Co., Inc., 1966.

————. *Obras Completas*. Madrid: Revista de Occidente, 1966.

————. *The Revolt of the Masses*. New York: W. W. Norton & Co., Inc., 1957.

Otto, Rudolf. *The Idea of the Holy*. New York: Oxford University Press, 1958.

Ovid. *Metamorphoses*, Rolfe Humphries, trans. Bloomington, IN: Indiana University Press, 1964.

Pascal, Blaise. *Pensées*. New York: E. P. Dutton & Co., 1958.

The Passion of Saints Perpetua and Felicitas, in *The Fathers of the Primitive Church*, Herbert A. Musurillo, ed. New York: Mentor, 1966.

Paulos, John Allen. *Mathematics and Humor*. Chicago: The University of Chicago Press, 1980.

Phenix, Philip, "Unamuno on Love and Pedagogy," in *Existentialism and Phenomenology in Education*, David E. Denton, ed. New York: Teachers College Press, 1974.

Phillips, John A. *Eve: The History of an Idea*. San Francisco: Harper & Row, 1984.

Philo of Alexandria. *Works of Philo, Complete and Unabridged*, C. D. Yonge, trans. Peabody, MA: Hendrickson Pub., 1993.

Piaget, Jean. *The Origins of Intelligence in Children*. New York: W. W. Norton & Co., 1963.

Pieper, Josef. *On Hope*, Mary M. McCarthy, trans. San Francisco: Ignatius Press, 1986.

Pirandello, Luigi. *On Humor*. Chapel Hill, NC: University of North Carolina Press, 1974.

Plato. *The Dialogues of Plato*, B. Jowett, trans. Oxford: Oxford University Press, 1871.

Prabhupāda, A. C. Bhaktivedanta Swami. *Krishna, The Supreme Personality of Godhead*. London: Bhaktivedanta Book Trust, 1986.

Rathor, Raghubir Singh. "Hamārī Samskriti aor Mahāsatyān," in *Mahāsatī Om Kanvar*. Jharli: Om Kanvar Trust, n. d.

Reps, Paul. *Zen Flesh, Zen Bones*. New York: Doubleday Anchor, n. d.

Robinson, James M., ed. *The Nag Hammadi Library*. San Francisco: Harper & Row, 1981.

Roper, William. "The Life of Sir Thomas More," in *The Harvard Classics*, Charles W. Eliot, ed. New York: P. F. Collier & Son Co., 1965.

Rosser, Barkley, "An Informal Exposition of Proofs of Gödel's Theorems and Church's Theorem," *The Journal of Symbolic Logic* 4:2 (June, 1939): 53-60.

Rothbart, Mary K. "Incongruity, Problem-solving, and Laughter," in *Humor and Laughter: Theory, Research, and Application*, Tony Chapman and Hugh Foot, eds. London: J. Wiley & Sons, 1976.

Rūmī, Jelaluddin. *Mathnawī*, R. A. Nicholson, trans. and ed. London: Luzac, 1925-1940.

Rümke, H. C. *The Psychology of Unbelief*. London: Rockliff, 1952.

Runde, Nan, "At Home in the Land of the Little Green Waiting-Maid." *Parabola* 26:3 (August, 2001).

Sagüés, Joseph F., S. J. *De Deo creante et elevante*, in *Sacrae Theologiae Summa*. Madrid: Biblioteca de autores Cristianos, 1958.

Salisbury, Joyce E. *Perpetua's Passion*. New York: Routledge, 1997.

Al- Sarrāj, Abū Nasr. *Kitāb al-Luma 'fī'l-Tasawwuf*, R. A. Nicholson, ed. Leyden: E. J. Brill, 1914.

Sartre, Jean-Paul. *Existentialism and Human Emotions*. New York: The Philosophical Library, 1957.

————. *The Imagination*. Ann Arbor: The University of Michigan Press, 1972.

————. *The Psychology of Imagination*. Secaucus, NJ: Citadel Press, 1972.

Scheeben, Matthias. *Mysteries of Christianity*. London: Herder & Herder, Co., 1946.

Scheffler, Israel. *Conditions of Knowledge*. Chicago: Scott, Foresman & Co., 1965.

Scheler, Max. *Ressentiment*. New York: Schocken Books, 1972.

Schopenhauer, Arthur. *Essays and Aphorisms*, R. J. Hollingdale, ed. London: Penguin Books, 1970.

————. *The World as Will and Representation*. Indian Hills, CO: The Falcon's Wing Press, 1958.

Schorske, Carl E. *Fin-de-Siècle Vienna: Politics and Culture*. New York: Alfred A. Knopf, 1980.

Shaw, George Bernard. *Collected Letters*, Dan H. Laurence, ed. New York: Viking, 1985.

Short, Robert L. *The Gospel According to Peanuts*. Richmond, VA: John Knox Press, 1965.

Shultz, Thomas R. "A Cognitive-developmental Analysis of Humor," in *Humor and Laughter: Theory, Research, and Application*, Tony Chapman and Hugh Foot, eds. London: J. Wiley & Sons, 1976.

Singer, Marcus G. *Generalization in Ethics*. New York: Alfred A. Knopf, 1961.

Smith, Huston. *Why Religion Matters*. San Francisco: HarperCollins, 2001.

Smullyan, Raymond M. *What is the Name of This Book?* Englewood Cliffs, NJ: Prentice-Hall, Inc., 1978.

Sorel, Georges. *Reflections on Violence*, T. E. Hulme, trans. New York: Collier Books, 1961.

Spinks, G. Stephens. *Psychology and Religion*. Boston: Beacon Press, 1967.

Spinoza, Benedict de. *Ethics*, in *Great Books of the Western World*, Robert M. Hutchins, ed. Chicago: Encyclopedia Britannica, 1952.

Stories from the Thousand and One Nights, Edward William Lane, trans. *The Harvard Classics*, Charles W. Eliot, ed. New York: P. F. Collier & Son Corp., 1965.

Suzuki, Daisetz Teitaro. *The Essentials of Zen Buddhism*. London: Rider & Co., 1962.

————. *Manual of Zen Buddhism*. New York: Grove Press, Inc., 1960.

————. *Sengai, the Zen Master*. New York: The New York Graphic Society, 1971.

Swift, Jonathan. *Gulliver's Travels*, in *Great Books of the Western World*, Robert M. Hutchins, ed. Chicago: Encyclopedia Britannica, 1952.

Tagore, Rabindranath. *Gitanjali*. London: Macmillan & Co., Ltd., 1966.

Tarski, Alfred, "The Semantic Conception of Truth," in *Problems in the Philosophy of Language*, Thomas M. Olshewsky, ed. New York: Holt, Rinehart & Winston, Inc., 1969.

Tarski, Alfred, Mostowski, Andrzej, and Robinson, Raphael M. *Undecidable Theories*. Amsterdam: North-Holland Publishing Co., 1968.

Teilhard de Chardin, Pierre. *The Phenomenon of Man*. New York: Harper & Row, 1961.

Tertullian. *Tertulliani Opera. Corpus Christianorum, series latina*. Turnhout: Brepols, 1954.

Tillich, Paul. *Dynamics of Faith*. New York: Harper Torchbooks, 1958.

————. *Systematic Theology*. Chicago: The University of Chicago Press, 1957.

Tolstoy, Leo. *War and Peace*, in *Great Books of the Western World*, ed. Robert M. Hutchins. Chicago: Encyclopaedia Britannica, 1952.

Travers, P. L., "Zen Moments." *Parabola* 12:4 (November, 1987).

Twain, Mark. "Captain Stormfield's Visit to Heaven," in *The Family Mark Twain*. New York: Harper & Row, 1972.

————. "Eve's Diary," in *The Family Mark Twain*. New York: Harper & Row, 1972.

————. *Pudd'nhead Wilson*, in *The Family Mark Twain*. New York: Harper & Row, 1972.

Unamuno, Miguel de. *Obras Completas*, Manuel García Blanco, ed. Madrid: Herederos de Miguel de Unamuno, 1965.

Valdés, Mario, and Valdés, María Elena de. *An Unamuno Source Book*. Toronto: University of Toronto Press, 1973.

Valmiki, *Rāmāyana*. Baroda: Oriental Institute, 1960-1975.

Van Ness, Peter H. *Spirituality, Diversion, and Decadence*. Albany: State University of New York Press, 1992.

Waismann, Friedrich. *The Principles of Linguistic Philosophy*. New York: St. Martin's Press, 1965.

Weinberger-Thomas, Catherine. *Ashes of Immortality: Widow-burning in India*. Chicago: The University of Chicago Press, 1999.

Wheelwright, Philip. *Heraclitus*. Princeton, NJ: Princeton University Press, 1959.

Williams, B. A. O. "Tertullian's Paradox," in *New Essays in Philosophical Theology*, A. N. Flew and A. MacIntyre, eds. New York: Macmillan, 1966.

Williams, John Alden. *Islam*. New York: George Braziller, 1962.

The Wisdom of Ben-Sira, W. O. E. Oesterley, ed. London: SPCK, 1916.

Wittgenstein, Ludwig. *Tractatus Logico-Philosophicus*. London: Routledge & Kegan Paul, 1961.

Woolman, John. *The Journal of John Woolman*, in *The Harvard Classics*, Charles W. Eliot, ed. New York: P. F. Collier & Son Corp., 1965.

Xenophon. *Cyropaedia*, G. Gemoll, trans. and ed. Cambridge: Oxford University Press, 1912.

Zaehner, R. C. *Hindu and Muslim Mysticism*. New York: Schocken Books, 1969.

Zeller, H. Van. *The Inner Search*. Garden City, NY: Image Books, 1967.

Zimmer, Heinrich. *Philosophies of India*. New York: Meridian, 1951.

Index

About the Author

IGNACIO L. GÖTZ is Lawrence Stessin Distinguished Professor and Teaching Fellow Emeritus at New College, Hofstra University. His books include *The Culture of
Sexism* (Praeger, 1999); *Manners and Violence* (Praeger, 2000); and *Technology and
the Spirit* (Praeger, 2001).